FROM **ANCIENT MESOPOTAMIA** AND THE
VIKING CONQUESTS TO **NATO** AND **WIKILEAKS,**
AN ESSENTIAL PRIMER ON WORLD HISTORY

WORLD HISTORY 101

TOM HEAD, PhD

Adams Media

New York   London   Toronto   Sydney   New Delhi

Adams Media
An Imprint of Simon & Schuster, Inc.
100 Technology Center Drive
Stoughton, MA 02072

First Adams Media hardcover edition OCTOBER 2017

ADAMS MEDIA and colophon are trademarks of Simon and Schuster.

For information about special discounts for bulk purchases, please contact Simon & Schuster Special Sales at 1-866-506-1949 or business@simonandschuster.com.

The Simon & Schuster Speakers Bureau can bring authors to your live event. For more information or to book an event contact the Simon & Schuster Speakers Bureau at 1-866-248-3049 or visit our website at www.simonspeakers.com.

Interior design by Michelle Kelly

Manufactured in Italy

10 9 8 7 6

Library of Congress Cataloging-in-Publication Data
Head, Tom, author.
World history 101 / Tom Head, PhD.
Avon, Massachusetts: Adams Media, 2017.
Series: 101
Includes index.
LCCN 2017026475 (print) | LCCN 2017028297 (ebook) | ISBN 9781507204542 (hc) | ISBN 9781507204559 (ebook)
LCSH: World history.
LCC D21 (ebook) | LCC D21 .H4276 2017 (print) | DDC 909--dc23
LC record available at https://lccn.loc.gov/2017026475

ISBN 978-1-5072-0454-2
ISBN 978-1-5072-0455-9 (ebook)

DEDICATION

In loving memory of my grandparents, Maybelle Bozeman Carwile
(1917–2011) and Robert Serrell Carwile (1907–1998), and to the billions of
ancestors—those who live on in our memories, and those too far away for
our memories to reach—who have given us all our history.

ACKNOWLEDGMENTS

To my wife Deirdre, who is sitting on the opposite side of the conference table in the office we share: Thank you for your patience and support during this writing process. I love you.

This book would not have been possible without my parents. Cappy and Carol Page-Head, without whom none of my books would have been written, and John Head, who has contributed more to my life than he may realize. They have and deserve my eternal gratitude.

To whatever extent I'm a reasonably well-adjusted person whose books are not an embarrassment to their publishers, my extended family also deserves some credit. To the Heads, the Pages, the Gannons, the Jacksons, the Garretts, the Myatts, and the Bennetts: thank you.

I owe a debt of thanks to my editor, Eileen Mullan, for making it possible for this book to go to press in the first place. This project also owes a great deal to developmental editor Peter Archer and copyeditor Mike van Mantgem; their strong sense of narrative and attention to detail were indispensable.

I will always be grateful to John and Mariah Bear, who helped me get started as a freelance writer seventeen years ago.

And like all historians working today, I owe a debt of gratitude to the late Rabbi Jacob Neusner (1932–2016), one of the most prolific scholars in history and—despite his unsurpassed productivity—among the most generous with his time. May his memory be a blessing.

CONTENTS

INTRODUCTION

"If history were taught in the form of stories,
it would never be forgotten."

—Rudyard Kipling (1865–1936)

History isn't just something we study; it's the story people collectively tell about themselves, both by their words and by their actions. Your birth, your death, and everything that happens in between is all part of history. It's true that most historians focus on political and military history, but that isn't because political and military history are more important than everything else; it's because this kind of history tends to leave a lot of *evidence* behind. As the great German playwright Bertolt Brecht (1898–1956) put it, kisses leave no traces but wounds leave scars. History is mostly about the scars.

This book tells the story of human beings, from the very beginning to the present. Each of its sixty-four chapters tells a story about a time and place in history with a few key dates and personalities singled out. A lot has been left out—the topic of world history is huge and there's always more to be said—but by the time you've finished this book, you'll have heard one version of the story of who we are and how we got here. And what a long, bumpy ride it has been.

A NOTE ON DATES

Most scholars now use B.C.E. (Before Common Era) instead of B.C. (Before Christ), and C.E. (Common Era) rather than A.D. (Anno Domini, which would be rendered in English as "in the year of our Lord"). I've adopted the scholarly habit in this book for several reasons—accuracy, mostly. The guy who came up with the B.C./A.D. dating system didn't know that Jesus was probably born sometime between 6 B.C.E. and 3 B.C.E. Simply stated, it's ridiculous to claim that Christ was born several years before Christ.

Although the B.C.E./C.E. distinction is more inclusive than B.C./A.D., and though it certainly *sounds* like the sort of new-fangled language scholars might have adopted in the past few decades, it has a much longer history than that. The German astronomer Johannes Kepler (1571–1630) used the Latin phrase for "Common Era," *vulgaris aerae*, as a substitute for anno Domini in his *Nova Stereometria* (1615).

HUMANITY BEFORE HISTORY

What the Bones Said

> "Did I request thee, Maker, from my clay
> To mould Me man? Did I solicit thee
> From darkness to promote me?"
> —John Milton (1608–1674), *Paradise Lost*, Book X

Today's humans are descended from scarce survivors of a global humanoid extinction. There were at one time *dozens* of humanoid species, among them Neanderthals, Denisovans, and "Hobbits," but at some point within the past fifty thousand years, starvation, disease, and violence have exterminated most of the humanoid family, leaving us only with ourselves. But our ancestors include untold members of these species, as well as the anatomically modern humans who knew them, mated with them, and competed with them for resources.

Stories of Creation

Almost every religious or cultural tradition in the world has an ancient, sacred story of how humanity came to exist. Regardless of their scientific accuracy, these stories have profound historical significance of their own.

As anatomically modern humans learned how to harness the power of agriculture, they settled into cities, city-states, and, ultimately, nations. Within these social institutions they began to keep permanent written records, records that make up source material for a broader human story. We call that story history.

MONUMENTS OF BONE

Figuring what happened before people wrote anything down, *before* history, is a difficult task. The most common view among scientists is that anatomically modern humans began appearing about two hundred thousand years ago in Ethiopia and much more recently spread from there throughout the world. Genetics tells us that all humans share a common ancestor and common genes. Some regional mutation occurred depending on climate, but the tidy division of human beings into genetically distinct races doesn't reflect the real history of our species. For most of human history, all our ancestors lived in the same general region and would have all been classified, by contemporary standards, as members of the same race.

The 195,000-year-old Omo fossils and 160,000-year-old Herto fossils are the oldest anatomically modern human remains ever found, and they reinforce the popular theory that our ancestors called Ethiopia home. But what did our ancestors *do* during these long ancient ages? What did they believe, how did they live, how did they speak, and how did they want to be remembered? While the Omo and Herto remains are often discussed together, as if these ancient people were contemporaries, we should pay attention to the fact that the 35,000-year gap in age between these two groups of fossils—a gap that otherwise reflects our total lack of knowledge regarding this part of the human story—is eight times as large as the gap between the beginning of recorded history and the present day. Human communities rose and fell during this period, for thousands and thousands of generations, and we know as little about them as they did about us. We are permanently separated from our first bold ancestors by the impenetrable curtain of time. We know more about our recent ancestors only because history gives us ways to pierce that curtain.

DIODORUS SICULUS WAS RIGHT

The Omo fossils were discovered in 1967, and until that time there was—as far as we know—no physical evidence suggesting that human beings originated in Ethiopia. So it's a little bit uncanny that *more than two thousand years earlier*, in his *Bibliotheca Historica*, the Greek author Diodorus Siculus (ca. 90–30 B.C.F.) had this to say about Ethiopia:

> "Now the Ethiopians, as historians relate, were the first of all men and the proofs of this statement, they say, are manifest. For that they did not come into their land as immigrants from abroad but were natives of it and so justly bear the name *autochthones* ['people of the earth'] is, they maintain, conceded by practically all men; furthermore, that those who dwell beneath the noon-day sun were, in all likelihood, the first to be generated by the earth, is clear to all; since, inasmuch as it was the warmth of the sun which, at the generation of the universe, dried up the earth when it was still wet and impregnated it with life, it is reasonable to suppose that the region which was nearest the sun was the first to bring forth living creatures."

Diodorus had almost certainly never even been to Ethiopia, and carbon dating wouldn't exist for millennia to come. But while his logic certainly doesn't hold up—we now know that Ethiopia is no closer to the sun than any other part of the world—his conclusion, which presumably reflected the conventional wisdom of the time, was accurate. And we have no idea why. It could have been a lucky guess, or an astonishingly well-preserved oral tradition, or just observation of ruins of old settlements that existed in ancient times but have since vanished. We don't know. We'll probably never know. History is full of little mysteries like that.

THE FIRST CITIES

Birds make nests, beavers make dams, and humans make camp. While the oldest discovered human settlements are "merely" tens of thousands of years old, we can assume—based on our knowledge of ourselves—that even the very first humans probably found environments they liked and customized them to meet their needs. While you don't need a city in order to have a political structure (most nomadic communities manage to create one just fine), you do need an urban environment in order to create the kind of permanent political structure that leaves enough material behind to create a historical record.

Given that fact, you may be surprised to learn that historians don't agree at all on what a city even *is*. The 21,000-year-old Ohalo II settlement in Israel, for example, meets most of the criteria we associate with cities: people lived there on a long-term basis, they had permanent huts, and there's evidence to suggest that they practiced agriculture (with more than a hundred seed varieties found onsite).

But the buildings weren't very durable and the human population at Ohalo II was most likely tiny, so it's generally called a village rather than a city. When we call an ancient settlement a city, we're not just saying that humans lived there; we're implying that it existed for a long enough period, and with enough stability, that it developed its own distinctive culture. Using that definition, among others, historians tend to believe that cities as we have come to know them have only existed for the past fifteen thousand years or so. For the vast majority of humanity's city-building history, all of the world's thriving cities could be found in one place: the fertile hinge connecting Africa, Asia, and Europe that we call the Middle East.

HUMAN CIVILIZATION IN SUMER AND AKKAD

The Cradle of History

> "That which I recited to you at midnight,
>   May the singer repeat it at noon!"
> —Enheduanna (ca. 2285–2250 B.C.E.), High Priestess of Ur,
>   as translated by W.W. Hallo and J.J.A. van Dijk

Human history began with cities, not nations. It was the mastery of agriculture that led people to settle down rather than migrating from place to place, and it was this settling down that led people to record their stories in writing, where it could be physically preserved, rather than through oral history alone. Few regions on Earth were more suitable for human agriculture five thousand years ago than the region historians call the Fertile Crescent. Also known as Mesopotamia (Greek for "between two rivers"), this area is located between the Tigris and Euphrates rivers in what we now call Iraq and Turkey. There, the people who called themselves the *sag-giga* ("black-headed people") founded and administered dozens of linked cities; produced copious amounts of literature, art, architecture, and music; and left behind the world's earliest known civilization. Only Egypt rivals it in age.

The broad outline of Mesopotamian history can be split into two periods: the time before 2300 B.C.E., when a loose alliance of city-states called Sumer spoke a single language and dealt collectively with natural, economic, and military challenges, and the period after 2300 B.C.E., when it was ruled over by a series of nations. The first of these nations, named after its city of origin, was Akkad.

IN THE DAYS OF SUMER

If you lived in Sumer during its early days, your life would probably have revolved around agriculture and the weather. In contrast to a modern city, where our food sources are stable and more or less invisible to us, the dozens of Sumerian cities scattered along flood plains of the Tigris and Euphrates operated more like today's rural communities: citizens knew where their food came from, and they were never more than one bad harvest away from famine. This made agreements among Sumerian cities crucial to their long-term survival.

Agreements were also necessary to deal with floods, a very real problem in these early riverside communities. After the cultural center of Shuruppak flooded near 3100 B.C.E., survivors and residents of neighboring cities talked about it, and the story was retold for over a thousand years—it was even said that Utnapishtim, the legendary Noah-figure who survived the flooding of the entire world, had served as governor of Shuruppak at the time.

But famine and natural disasters were not the only threats Sumerians faced. Alliances were also necessary to deter war. Archaeologists have uncovered mysterious ruins they call Hamoukar, located not far from Uruk, which was clearly once a city. At some point around 3500 B.C.E., Hamoukar came under siege by the heaviest artillery available at the time. Clay slingshot pellets tore holes in the city's walls and internal structures and would have been deadly for any human targets in their path. We still don't know who invaded Hamoukar or why, and surviving Sumerian literature has no clear record of the incident, but it speaks to the dangers every city faced if it didn't prepare itself for war.

Gudea of Lagash

If you've ever seen a statue of a Sumerian, it was probably that of the governor and social reformer Gudea, who ruled Lagash for twenty years starting around 2144 B.C.E. Gudea instituted a variety of building projects and social reforms in his home city-state, including allowing women to inherit property.

THROUGH MANY, ONE

Although Sumer had a series of *lugals* ("kings"), these were generally the governors of specific city-states who were given regional diplomatic powers. No city-states entirely monopolized this authority—it was not uncommon to have a lugal from one city and then a lugal from another—and the pathways to power were often unorthodox. Kubaba of Kish, the only female lugal mentioned in the Sumerian Kings List, is said to have ascended to leadership by selling the finest beer in Sumer—an early example of a political figure achieving power by leveraging her private-sector success.

This apparently friendly and practical arrangement among city-states seems to have remained stable for a very long time; if we assume it began with the founding of Eridu around 5400 B.C.E., it would have lasted some three thousand years—far longer than any of the empires that followed. So it certainly wasn't a failure. But there's little reason for a cluster of self-sustaining city-states to raise up a large army, a weakness the aspiring emperor Sargon I is said to have exploited at some point around 2334 B.C.E., conquering Sumer under the banner of his home city-state of Akkad. The Akkadians were not the only empire to rule over Mesopotamia, but they were the first, and their rise marked the end of Sumer as we know it. After Sargon, the only kind of peace the leaders of Mesopotamia could give their people was peace through strength.

The Epic of Gilgamesh

The national hero of Sumer was Gilgamesh, the legendary king of Uruk whose quest for immortality is the subject of the world's oldest surviving epic poem. But there wasn't just *one* story about Gilgamesh; like King Arthur or Robin Hood, he was imagined and reimagined for centuries by a series of storytellers who described his adventures with his lover and sidekick, the heroic beast-man Enkidu.

THE FIRST HALF OF EGYPT'S STORY

The Children of Osiris

"Thou art born, O Horus, as one whose name is 'Him at whom the earth quakes'…
No seed of a god, which belongs to him, goes to ruin;
so thou who belongest to him will not go to ruin."

—The *Pyramid Texts*, Utterance 215

Egypt is the world's oldest surviving civilization. Egypt's first few thousand years are known mainly for its pyramids, as the scale and durability of these monuments are awe inspiring, but there was a time when ancient Egypt was not that different from the nation of the same name today—a bright, noisy, diverse living society full of stories and intrigue, economics and war, beauty and horror.

Civilizations never start off as civilizations. Like Sumer, Egypt sprouted from a cluster of river settlements. Sumer had the Tigris and Euphrates, and Egypt had the Nile.

THE HAWK AND THE VULTURE

Egypt, like Sumer, began with cities. Over time, these cities coalesced into two kingdoms: Lower Egypt, whose national symbol was the god Horus, represented by the hawk, and Upper Egypt, whose symbol was the vulture-headed goddess Nekhbet. At some point around 3000 B.C.E., a king identified as Menes is said to have united the two kingdoms forever, becoming the first pharaoh to rule over all of Egypt.

The idea of the pharaoh is a hard one for contemporary readers to wrap their heads around. Looking at the opulent tombs they were buried in, and contrasting this with the relatively simple structures and finite resources that surrounded them, we may be tempted to view them as symbols of decadence. But it's important to remember that the pharaohs, born into dynasties of rulers, were raised to believe they really were the conduits between the gods, who represented primal cosmic forces, and the people around them. The pharaoh, tasked with protecting Egypt's mortals from forces both human and divine, could not have easily rejected the trappings of this role without offending the gods—and, obviously, could not have rejected posthumous honors at all.

Ma'at

The most central moral value in ancient Egyptian religion is *ma'at* (pronounced "may-at"), or order. The idea is that by being honest and straightforward, and living in harmony with reality and each other, we can improve the world in this life and our prospects for the world to come.

One of the more unsettling elements of Egyptian iconography, for today's audiences, may be the tendency to portray gods with the bodies of humans and the heads of animals. But it's important to remember that for ancient Egyptians there was no distinction between the gods and natural forces. The lion-headed goddess Tefnut *was* goddess of rain, for example, but she was also the personification of rain. All rain was attributable to Tefnut. So rather than portraying her as human, it was important to portray her as something wild. The human connection with the gods, the human intermediary between the world of mortals and the world of gods, was the pharaoh.

TOMBS OF THE IMMORTALS

Ancient Egypt was one of the first civilizations to intentionally mummify corpses, but this wasn't originally an honor reserved for the pharaohs. After burying the dead in ordinary graves, the people of Egypt noticed that bodies buried in the dry desert were better-preserved than bodies buried in moist ground. Correctly surmising a relationship between dryness and preservation, the priestly class of Egypt soon perfected the art of keeping corpses dry and free of rot, preserving their leaders' bodies as a sign of their spiritual incorruptibility.

For similar reasons, early pharaohs were buried with living servants who were sacrificed in this world, and buried with their pharaohs, to serve them in the next. In apparent recognition that this policy was inhumane, later pharaohs were buried with small *shabti* statues intended to depict their servants in the world to come.

Today the mummification of pharaohs has allowed contemporary scientists to perform X-rays, genetic tests, and other experiments to help them better understand who the people of ancient Egypt were and what their lives were like. The tombs, once a symbol of how much the people loved the pharaohs, now provide the most comprehensive trove of artifacts we have by which to understand ancient Egyptian art, technology, and culture. In that respect, the pharaohs of ancient

Egypt have become, in a very literal sense, exactly what their people wanted them to be: immortal conduits between their world and the next.

The Great Pyramid

No monument represents the pharaoh's eternal role more clearly, and more enduringly, than the 138 stone pyramids that dot the Egyptian landscape. The greatest of these is the 4,600-year-old Great Pyramid of Giza, the tomb of the pharaoh Khufu (ca. 2600–2528 B.C.E.), which still stands and, unless it is intentionally destroyed by human hands, is likely to stand for many thousands of years to come. At 481 feet tall and about 756 feet long on each side, it is the largest surviving monument of the ancient world and is still impressive by contemporary standards—big enough to be easily seen from the International Space Station, if one has a general idea of where to look. It would be extremely difficult to build a full-scale replica today, and the amount of labor and ingenuity involved in constructing it using the tools of the ancient world remain unfathomable. It wasn't just a work of genius, a work of art; it was a work of devotion and love for the dead, and its longevity is an enduring act of defiance against death itself.

MEGACITIES OF THE ANCIENT INDUS VALLEY

Ancient History Carved in Stone

"Whence all creation had its origin,
he, whether he fashioned it or whether he did not,
he, who surveys it all from highest heaven,
he knows—or maybe even he does not know."
—From the "Hymn of Creation" (Rig-Veda 10:129), translated by A.L. Basham

---

As the complex network of Sumerian city-states began to achieve regional dominance in Mesopotamia, mysterious communities living two thousand miles east on the Indian subcontinent began to construct massive stone cities to accommodate a growing population. Ultimately abandoned, these cities provide archaeologists and historians with a glimpse into the early centuries of one of the world's most powerful and diverse civilizations.

Hindu tradition has its own stories of the origins of India, tales of an Emperor Bharata who left behind a mighty civilization. Do the ancient cities of Mehrgarh and Mohenjo-daro suggest that these historical accounts have a basis in reality?

EPICS AND MYSTERIES

Like most ancient civilizations the society of the Indus Valley civilization was identified with a river. Even the name we give the country today—India, derived from Indus—comes from the Sanskrit term *Sindhu*, which refers in a general sense to any large body of water and in a specific sense to the massive Ganges river. The word *Hindu* comes from the same root word. To the extent that we call it India, it is a country that—much like the US states of Mississippi and Missouri—is named after a distinctive river.

For most residents of India, the country has a different name: Bharat. The word has a general meaning—to keep a fire lit—and in that sense Bharat is the fire that is protected, and kept burning, by the people and their rulers. In much the same way that America was named after the explorer and mapmaker Amerigo Vespucci, Bharat is said to have been named after the ancient mythical Emperor Bharata, who inherited a united India and kept that fire burning. The broad outline of his life is described in the *Mahabharata*, the massive and ancient epic poem of India.

Not a Post-Nuclear Wasteland

The History Channel television series *Ancient Aliens* made the argument that the city of Mohenjo-daro was destroyed by a nuclear explosion, citing the fact that pottery found at the site had vitrified due to high heat. But vitrification is a normal part of the clay-firing process, and the relatively well-preserved state of the site—which included intact mud buildings and walls—seems to preclude a large catastrophic explosion of any kind.

If there's a historical figure who inspired this story of Bharata, he would have almost certainly been found in the ancient civilization of the Indus Valley. Operating from about 6000 B.C.E. until around 1500 B.C.E., it was one of the oldest civilizations in the world. It was also among the most advanced, and the cities—often intricately designed, and featuring impressive amenities like indoor plumbing and public swimming pools—are still studied by urban planners to this day. But it's what we don't know about this ancient civilization that tends to captivate the people who study it.

The World's Greatest Detectives

Historians are good at putting together disparate documentary evidence. But when you don't have reliable documentary evidence to work with, piecing together a timeline depends entirely on the work of archaeologists—the CSIs of historical research. By locating, collecting, and preserving physical evidence, they can reconstruct stories that would otherwise be lost to time.

The case of the Indus Valley civilization is particularly hard because their language has not yet been deciphered. The Indus Valley script that archaeologists have found in these ancient cities bears some superficial similarities to other scripts from the region, but not enough to piece together the meaning of the short lines. Some experts have suggested that the Indus Valley language might not be a true language at all—that it may be, instead, a series of personalized seals that serve the same purpose as a signature or brand logo. Nobody knows for certain yet.

So it's the cities themselves that have to do the talking, and what they tell us is that thousands of years ago a civilization thrived in India and Pakistan. This civilization rivaled Sumer in size, and it traded with its better-known rivals to the distant west. Over time, from these beginnings, classical India—one of the most powerful and influential civilizations that has ever existed—came to be.

Nazis Ruin Everything

The Third Reich borrowed multiple innocuous symbols from ancient India and permanently changed their meaning. The swastika, for example, was originally a common Hindu symbol often meant to indicate good luck, a blessing, or sanctuary. The Nazis also borrowed the Sanskrit root word *arya*, which means "unique" or "important," and made it an explicit racial reference with the term "Aryan."

THE HITTITES AND WHAT THEY LEFT BEHIND

The Empire Strikes First

> "Until now, no member of my family has obeyed my will."
> —From the political testament of the Hittite king Hattusili I
> (ca. 1586–1556 B.C.E.)

For most of human history, we have lived in relatively small groups—tribes, settlements, and, later, cities. But in recent centuries these smaller groups have clumped together in, or been absorbed (often forcibly) by, larger nations and empires. By 1300 B.C.E., this pattern had already been established in the region that hosted the world's oldest civilizations: the Middle East. In the north were the Hittites, in the south were the New Kingdom Egyptians, and to the southeast were the Assyrians (both discussed later).

The Hittites were, for a time, the most powerful of the three empires, dominating the Egyptians and looting Babylon outright. Their armored chariots were the tanks of the ancient world, dominant in combat, fast enough for raids and reconnaissance, and a powerful symbol of law and order in conquered cities. But there's a reason history books don't talk about them much: They were a force to be reckoned with for only a few centuries. By 1200 B.C.E. the Hittite agricultural system had collapsed and they depended on Egypt for grain shipments; a few decades later, their capital Hattusa would fall to the Assyrians. But for a time, a considerably long time, their power was unmatched.

The Three Empires of the Middle East, ca. 1300 B.C.E.

Thirty-three hundred years ago, the Middle East was dominated by three superpowers: the Hittites in the north, the Egyptians in the south, and the Assyrians in the southeast.

THE PHARAOH'S WIDOW

One story that sums up the power of the Hittites, at their peak, is about a Hittite prince who almost became pharaoh of Egypt. And it all started with Tutankhamen's death.

Historians have long speculated that the pharaoh Tutankhamen was murdered. Whether he was or not, a shroud of suspicion surrounded his death at the time—so much so that Hittite records tell the story of the pharaoh's widow, most likely Tut's widow, Ankhesenamun, visiting the Hittite king Suppiluliuma in 1325 B.C.E. with an unusual request: "My husband has died and I have no son....You might give me one of your sons to become my husband. I would not wish to take one of my subjects as a husband....I am afraid."

Suppiluliuma sent Ankhesenamun home with his son Zannanza. As it turned out, Ankhesenamun's suspicions were well-founded; according to Hittite records, Zannanza was murdered by Egyptian officials, worsening relations between the two nations. The dream of an Egyptian-Hittite royal marriage was finally realized a century later, when Pharaoh Rameses II married the Hittite princess Maathorneferure.

The Oldest Music in the World

The Hurrian hymn to Nikkal, also known as "Hurrian Hymn No. 6," is the oldest surviving piece of sheet music—and, therefore, the oldest melody in the world (though musicologists are still not entirely sure they've rendered it correctly).

THE PHARAOHS OF EGYPT'S NEW KINGDOM

Look upon My Works, Ye Mighty, and Despair

> "I have restored that which was in ruins.
> I have raised up that which was unfinished."
> —Hatshepsut (ca. 1507–1458 B.C.E.), pharaoh of Egypt

History tends to judge civilizations by what they've left behind. By that standard, few civilizations—ancient or modern—have a legacy as impressive as that of ancient Egypt, which gave us the Great Pyramids (they have stood for over 4,500 years and will no doubt outlast us all), numerous smaller but similarly impressive sculptures and specialized temples, and a fairly large body of religious and wisdom literature written in that civilization's distinctive hieroglyphic language.

All of this already existed by 1300 B.C.E., when Egypt's pharaohs ruled alongside their rivals the Hittites to the north and the Assyrians to the east. By this point, Egypt was already an unfathomably ancient nation full of histories, mysterious traditions, and landmarks whose original purpose had already been forgotten. But these pharaohs of the Eighteenth, Nineteenth, and Twentieth dynasties, who ruled from about 1549 B.C.E. until 1077 B.C.E., saw—correctly, as it turns out—an Egypt that was still young, and that still had a boundless future ahead of it. Historians call this period the New Kingdom era, and they look back on it as one of several golden ages in Egypt's long and impressive history.

HORIZON OF THE ATEN

Ancient Egyptian religion was historically a balanced polytheism; priests and commoners worshipped a diverse pantheon of gods and goddesses, each with their own destinies, local histories, and spheres of influence. The pharaoh Akhenaten, who ruled from about 1353 B.C.E. until about 1336 B.C.E., felt especially strongly about the sun god Aten, who represented—he believed—a fundamental force in the cosmos. Although historians often describe Akhenaten as a monotheist, that wasn't exactly right; he believed other gods existed. They just didn't hold a candle to Aten. Aten was something special, something fundamental to the nature of reality itself. This belief in the supremacy of one god over other gods is generally called henotheism. Akhenaten's insistence of having no other gods before Aten may have influenced countless other religions, including ultimately those of Judaism, Christianity, and Islam.

Hatshepsut

The pharaoh Hatshepsut, who ruled for twenty years (ca. 1478 B.C.E. to 1458 B.C.E.), was one of the first female pharaohs. Like many women of prominence throughout history, she was subjected to a posthumous effort to erase her achievements and credit them to her male successor. It didn't work.

By the standards of the time this belief was also wildly controversial. The controversy was compounded when Akhenaten moved the capital of the Egyptian empire from ancient Thebes to Amarna, a new city he ordered constructed two hundred sixty miles to the north in tribute to Aten. For a decade the city of Amarna was a place of new innovations in urban planning, art, and architecture. But the city did not endure. Thebes became the capital again after Akhenaten's death. Because Amarna was later abandoned, it provided archaeologists with a near-pristine ancient city to uncover some three thousand years later.

What Remains of Rameses

In 1818 the British poets Percy Bysshe Shelley and Horace Smith decided to write competing poems about recently uncovered ancient monuments in honor of Ozymandias, the name the Greeks gave to the pharaoh Rameses II, who reigned from about 1279 B.C.E. until 1213 B.C.E. Shelley's poem, by far the more famous of the two, reads in part:

"Two vast and trunkless legs of stone
Stand in the desert...Near them, on the sand,
Half sunk, a shattered visage lies, whose frown,
And wrinkled lip, and sneer of cold command,
Tell that its sculptor well those passions read
Which yet survive, stamped on these lifeless things,
The hand that mocked them and the heart that fed:
And on the pedestal these words appear:
'My name is Ozymandias, king of kings:
Look on my works, ye Mighty, and despair!'
Nothing beside remains."

This is the message contemporary readers tend to take from the legacy of Rameses II: that power is arrogant and ephemeral. But a cursory review of ancient Egyptian literature suggests that the Egyptians of three thousand years ago were already keenly aware of the insubstantial nature of human achievement. These monuments, these tombs, these mummies were not necessarily meant to escape the passage of time but rather to provide future generations with a past they could find, a past whose shadow would loom over them and offer them guidance. As archaeologists continue to study ancient Egypt thousands of years later, the pharaohs continue to guide posterity and provide humanity with permanent symbols of history, in more impressive and far-reaching ways than even they could have planned.

The Tomb of Nefertiti

Archaeologists believe they may have successfully located the long-lost tomb of Queen Nefertiti, wife to the pharaoh Akhenaten, in a secret underground burial chamber linked to the tomb of her son Tutankhamen. They won't know for certain until they can excavate it.

THE MARSH EMPIRES OF MESOPOTAMIA

By the Waters of Babylon

> "I am Sennacherib,
> king of Assyria, the prince who reveres thee.
> He who erases my written name
> or alters this, your seal of Destinies—
> erase his name
> and his seed from the land."
> —From the seal of Sennacherib (ca. 740–681 B.C.E.),
> as translated by D.J. Wiseman

In 1300 B.C.E., as the Hittites dominated the region we now call Turkey, and the New Kingdom ruled over Egypt, the Assyrians ruled over northern Mesopotamia. Although they still spoke the Akkadian language and originated in the northern Sumerian cities, the Assyrians were very different from the Mesopotamian civilizations that preceded them—more uniform, more efficient, more brutal.

In southern Mesopotamia, a rival empire—centered in Babylon—ebbed and flowed in relative power from about 1830 B.C.E. until 539 B.C.E. At times it dominated Assyria, at times it was dominated by Assyria, but it never entirely won or—until the end—entirely lost the struggle for Mesopotamia.

THE ASSYRIAN CONTRADICTION

In some respects no ancient empire was more like a modern super-power than the Assyrians—they ruthlessly dominated puppet king-doms with violence and violent threats, while at the same time their empire served as an international center of learning and culture. Emerging from the ancient city-state of Assur in northern Mesopota-mia, the Assyrians ruled the region intermittently from about 2000 B.C.E. until the fall of its metropolis, Nineveh, in 612 B.C.E.

And they were terrifying. No ancient empire was more brutal than the Assyrians. "I flayed as many nobles as had rebelled against me," Ashurnasirpal wrote after conquering the city of Suru in 678 B.C.E. "Some I erected on stakes....I flayed many right through my land and draped their skins over the walls." The nobles knew this punishment was coming; the vassal treaties that Assyrian kings required member cities to sign promised similarly gruesome fates to any who rebelled.

Cuneiform

Literate scribes among the Sumerians, Akkadians, Assyrians, and Babylonians all primarily wrote on clay tablets using a *cuneiform* (Latin for "wedge-form") alphabet. These scribes were basically the attorneys of their time, using their liter-acy to keep public records and verify the authenticity of contracts. But they also transcribed letters, laws, hymns, wisdom literature, and even works of fiction.

Yet the Assyrians hosted the world's largest library in Nineveh, had some of the most sophisticated plumbing systems in the ancient world, and were the first major empire to create a network of road stations for rapid communication. They were unmatched patrons of the arts, had a sophisticated state religion, and drew on thousands of years of culture and tradition.

The Assyrians were, in other words, both deeply barbaric *and* deeply civilized. In the history of the world it has not been uncommon for a nation to display both traits, but none embody this contradiction as clearly, and as shamelessly, as Assyria.

Mighty Babylon

By most accounts Babylon was to the ancient Middle East what New York City, Las Vegas, and New Orleans are to North America. Like New York City, it was an unimaginably vast and impressive economic powerhouse; like Las Vegas, it was a visually stunning center of tourism and sin; and like New Orleans, it was an old city with a distinct culture and a million secret stories to tell.

Most of the things we popularly associate with ancient Mesopotamia came from the ancient Babylonian Empire, not other civilizations. It was Hammurabi (ca. 1810–1750 B.C.E.), the sixth ruler of the first Babylonian Empire, who gave us the infamous ancient code that promised an eye for an eye. It was also the Babylonian Empire that gave us the mad king Nebuchadnezzar II (ca. 634–562 B.C.E.), whose dreams were central to the Book of Daniel. Babylon is said to have given us one of the Seven Wonders of the Ancient World—the Hanging Gardens—and it remains, in Judaism and Christianity, a potent symbol of worldly power. Babylon's own religion, centering on the gods Tiamat and Marduk, is the one to which contemporary texts most commonly refer when they speak of ancient Mesopotamian religion.

Despite all of this it's easy to overlook the Babylonian Empire. It was neither as ancient as Sumer nor as brutal or architecturally impressive as Assyria. It's neither as famously well-preserved as Egypt nor as famously obscure and misunderstood as the empire of the Hittites. But for more than a millennium, during a series of golden ages punctuated by short-term collapses, Babylon represented the legacy of those ancient southern Mesopotamian cities that were the cradle of civilization itself.

The Five Books of Moses

The Babylonian Empire may be indirectly responsible for Jewish scribes' decision to write down the Hebrew Bible (also known as the Christian Old Testament), as they had captured Israel and exiled its priests in 587 B.C.E.

THE ANCIENT WORLD OF THE OLMECS

Where the Rubber Met the Road

"What, precisely, was their social structure? Who were their gods and what powers did they wield? These questions and many others are still unanswered. Olmec archaeology is still a young science and even though the Olmec lands are generously endowed with mute testimonials to further it, a series of circumstances has prevented its development at the same speed as other related branches during our present century."
—Beatriz de la Fuente (1929–2005), Mesoamerican art historian

---

While mighty empires struggled over control of the Middle East, a new culture began to take shape in the jungles of Mesoamerica around 1500 B.C.E. and dominated the region until it disappeared, to be replaced by later empires, about a thousand years later.

Because no Olmec texts have been translated, we know very little about them. To begin with, they probably didn't call themselves the Olmecs; it was the Aztec term for them and could be loosely translated as "the rubber people." It's also highly unlikely, given the vast amount of time involved, that they were just one civilization that lasted a thousand years. But whoever they were, and whatever they did, they left behind massive cities, impressive sculptures, and a permanently unresolvable mystery.

THE RUBBER PEOPLE

There is strong archaeological evidence to suggest that more than three thousand years ago the Olmecs played some version of *ulama*, the sacred Mesoamerican ball game later adopted by the Mayans and Aztecs. Ulama wasn't for the squeamish; unlike the inflatable rubber balls used in Western sports, Olmec rubber balls were solid and weighed up to ten pounds. Considering the speed that the balls were likely to have traveled, this almost certainly would have dramatically increased the risk of sport-related injury.

WHEN GIANTS WALKED

Olmec civilization is most often remembered today for the seventeen massive, multiton carved basalt heads it left behind. These heads are intricate enough that they are probably intended to represent specific people, though who exactly they're intended to portray is a mystery whose answer is long since lost to time.

Thousands of years later Aztec texts would teach that an extinct race of giants, the Quinametzin, was responsible for creating many of the region's most impressive cities and architectural marvels. Was this story inspired by the Olmecs themselves, by the colossal sculptures they left behind, or by unrelated Aztec legends?

There may be a way to find out what the Olmecs themselves thought. In 1999 construction workers digging through old rubble in a village near Veracruz, Mexico, discovered a 14-inch stone tablet with unfamiliar symbols on it. Dubbed the Cascajal stone, the tablet could be a surviving artifact of the ancient Olmec world; the village sits on ancient Olmec ruins that had already been dated to approximately 900 B.C.E., and the symbols on the tablet do not correspond to known Mesoamerican languages. Linguists are hard at work decoding it. But even if the Cascajal block itself turns out to be of a more recent vintage than the Olmecs, its discovery highlights just how much of the region has been unexplored. The Olmecs' own story could still lie buried under undisturbed ground, the silent record of a world made alien by time.

Legends of the Ancient Giants

As is a common characteristic of ancient myths, Aztec stories of the Quinametzin echo similar stories told in other parts of the world. In Genesis 6:4, its ancient Israeli writers tell us about the Nephilim, a race of giants said to have walked the earth prior to the Great Flood. Ancient Greek poets wrote in turn about the Titans, ancient giants who were said to have predated most of the gods themselves.

CYRUS THE GREAT AND THE ACHAEMENID DREAM

The Persian Messiah

"Thus saith the Lord to his anointed, to Cyrus, whose right hand I have holden, to subdue nations before him; and I will loose the loins of kings, to open before him the two leaved gates; and the gates shall not be shut..."

—Isaiah 45:1 (KJV)

Living in captivity in Babylon under the yoke of the brutal Assyrians, the priests of ancient Israel faced a difficult decision in 587 B.C.E: either write down a permanent record of their faith's teachings or watch those teachings die with them. They chose the former, and we have the Hebrew Bible, more often known as the Christian Old Testament, to show for it. The text often aches with injustice, as in Psalm 137: "By the rivers of Babylon, we sat and wept when we remembered Zion."

But the Hebrew Bible also contains a hopeful message of a mighty king who would come to save the Jewish people: Cyrus the Great of Persia, who is said to have lived from about 590 B.C.E. until about 530 B.C.E. Although he was not a Jew, belonging instead to the ancient Persian religion Zoroastrianism, he is identified clearly and explicitly in Hebrew as a messiah—a saving instrument of God himself. And when Cyrus conquered Babylon in 539 B.C.E., he fully lived up to their expectations. The priests returned home to Israel stronger in their faith, and armed with Scripture.

THUS SPOKE ZARATHUSTRA

In order to understand why Cyrus was so good for Israel, it's important to remember what his own religious beliefs told him: that the world is locked in a constant struggle between a good deity, the benevolent creator, Ahura Mazda, and his evil son, Ahriman, the father of lies. According to Zoroastrianism, it doesn't really matter all that much which religion you personally belong to; what matters is that you're on the right side of this struggle. So while Zoroastrians welcomed converts, they didn't demand conversion—and they allowed the civilizations they conquered to continue to practice their local faiths.

Zoroaster

The founder of Zoroastrianism is said to have been the prophet Zoroaster, also known as Zarathustra, who preached that the deadliest cosmic force—and the one that gives power to Ahriman—is *druj* (a lie). According to Zoroaster, telling the truth when it matters can save the world.

By the standards of the sixth century B.C.E., this was an incredibly radical idea. Historically, religion was used to unite a civilization and impose a civic creed on its subjects. To deny the divinity of the pharaoh was to deny the legitimacy of the Egyptian government; to deny the priestesses of ancient Sumer meant denying the divinely sanctioned authority of each city's rulers; and so forth. The Persians sacrificed this opportunity to merge church and state, predating Western democracies' attempts to do so by millennia, creating in the process a diverse, stable empire in which differences of opinion were relatively commonplace and relatively welcome.

Expanding from their homeland in Persia, known today as Iran, the Persians changed the way emperors ruled their subjects. Gone was the certainty that every civilization under an empire's control always must conform to imperial culture and religion, though this remained the norm. The Persian Empire set a better example—albeit one that few Western or Middle Eastern civilizations would make any serious attempt to follow.

The United States of Ancient Persia

While ancient Persia could be best understood as an absolute divine right monarchy, in many other respects it better conforms to the values we associate with modern liberal democracies than most of its rivals. The Persian Empire prohibited slavery, allowed women to own property, granted considerable local autonomy to conquered states, prioritized education and trade, and permitted an unprecedented level of religious freedom. In terms of basic human rights it is a far more accurate precursor to modern states than ancient Greece could ever have been.

But these two civilizations are seldom presented in this way; this is more or less a legacy of the Crusades. For a millennium, Americans and other Westerners have been encouraged by some in Western media to see the world as the seat of an ideological struggle between the Christian West and the Islamic Middle East. Although the ancient Greeks were pagan rather than Christian, and the Persians were Zoroastrian rather than Muslim, historians have subtly projected this idea of the Crusades on the Persian-Greek conflict.

A particularly egregious example of this can be found in the 2006 film *300*, based on a 1998 comic book of the same name. It portrayed the Persians as bloody-minded, rapacious monsters and their Greek foes as brave and honorable underdogs. In practice, both civilizations contributed in significant and irreplaceable ways to the world we've inherited.

Achaemenes

We've tried to avoid using the long and unwieldy word *Achaemenid* in this chapter, but that's what the Persian Empire of this era was called by the Greeks (and, subsequently, by most Western historians). It takes its name from Achaemenes, an ancient mythical hero from whom the Persian dynasty was said to have descended.

THE SECRETS OF KUSH

The Triumph of Ancient Ethiopia and Sudan

"Only yesterday Zeus went off to the Ocean River
to feast with the Ethiopians, loyal, lordly men,
and all of the gods went with him."
—Thetis in Homer's *The Iliad*, Book I, verses 423–424

As we talked about in the chapter Humanity Before History, the story of humanity began about two hundred thousand years ago in Ethiopia. Given that fact, you'd think we would know more about that country's ancient history than we do. You would suppose we'd be reading ancient Ethiopian literature, studying ancient Ethiopian religions, and so on. Two factors confound our efforts to do that: there aren't very many surviving documents from ancient Ethiopia, and we can't read most of the ones we do have.

Ethiopians during the Kush period wrote a script we call Meroitic, named after the city of Meroë. Despite more than a century of study, we still can't read it. The good news is that there's a better than even chance that we will one day learn how to read Meroitic, either because we find a Meroitic translation of a text from another language (or vice versa) or because one of the many linguists working to untangle the puzzle of this long-mysterious language figures it out on her or his own. But for now, Kush's greatest mysteries are hidden from us.

THE SOUTHERN PHARAOHS

Kush was a really busy place. Located just to the south of Egypt, and comprising both Sudan and Ethiopia (which were often referred to collectively by classical historians as Ethiopia), it was a hub for regional politics and trade—connecting the northern world of the Mediterranean to the southern world of sub-Saharan nations. And as little as we know about Kush, we know even less about most of the southern nations it interacted with. There's evidence beginning in the fourth century B.C.E. of an astonishingly high amount of cross-cultural contact with somebody who influenced dramatic changes in the Meroitic language and carried over a new pantheon of gods who weren't part of the traditional Egyptian-influenced Kushite pantheon. We can reasonably assume that these changes probably came about due to contact with an ancient sub-Saharan nation we still don't know anything about. If we ever learn to read Meroitic, this may be one of the many mysteries solved by the surviving documents in that language.

One thing we do know a lot about is contact between the ancient Ethiopian nations and Egypt, whose records were far better preserved. At different times the ancient Kushite kingdom both conquered and was conquered *by* Egypt, but most of their interactions were more peaceful and mutually beneficial than that.

We also have scattered references to Ethiopian society from Greek literature, most of which describes the Kushite kingdom as an earthly paradise. The historian of record was Diodorus Siculus (ca. 90–30 B.C.E.), whom we mentioned in the first chapter. He was the first known author to propose (correctly, as we now know, based on radiocarbon dating of the oldest known human remains) that humanity originated in Ethiopia. Although many of his theories seem far-fetched—such as the claim that the Kushites fought and defeated the mythical Hercules, or that the Egyptian god Osiris was actually an Ethiopian who founded the kingdom of Egypt as a settler—it's unclear as to whether they reflect oral traditions that originated in the Kushite kingdom or if they just reveal the capacity of Diodorus's own imagination.

THE BIBLICAL KUSH

There is a Kush mentioned in the Hebrew Bible (and usually rendered in English Bibles as "Cush") that is almost certainly a reference of some kind to the Kushite kingdom, though it may also be a more general geographical reference. The most prominent references to Kush are as follows:

- In the Table of Nations (Genesis 10:6), Kush is identified as one of the allegorical nations descended from Noah's son Ham. During segregationist eras in the United States and South Africa, many white clergy used Kush's status as a child of the cursed son Ham as an excuse to argue for black racial inferiority.
- Nimrod of Kush, a "mighty hunter before the Lord" and early Mesopotamian founder, is briefly mentioned (Genesis 10:8–10). Geographically this does not seem to be a reference to the Kushite region, which is on the opposite side of the Arabian Peninsula from Mesopotamia, but it could be.
- Numbers 12 makes reference to Moses marrying a Kushite woman (named Zipporah), and God punishing Moses' brother and sister for objecting to the union.

- Jeremiah 13:23 reads, "Can a Kushite change his skin, or a leopard its spots?" This passage suggests that the biblical Kushites—or at least the Kushites referred to in this verse—had a skin color distinctively different than that of the Israelites, which would make sense if they hailed from Sudan and Ethiopia, as their skin would be noticeably darker.

Most biblical scholars suspect that Kush is sometimes a specific reference to the Kushite region, and sometimes a more general reference to civilizations that settled along the Red Sea.

Candace

Although Meroitic is mostly a mystery to us, one word—by way of Greek—has made its way into English: the name Candace, derived from the title Kushites used for their queens (*kandake*).

HOW THE GREEK CITY-STATES UNITED

Hellas and High Water

"I declare
That later on,
Even in an age unlike our own,
Someone will remember who we are."
—Sappho of Lesbos (610–570 B.C.E.), poet

It's hard to overstate the importance of ancient Greece to the history of the world and the West in particular, but that hasn't stopped some people from trying. To hear some thinkers of the eighteenth and nineteenth centuries say it, the people of Greece had it all figured out two millennia ago. That's not even remotely true, but what ancient Greece did accomplish in terms of science, architecture, literature, art, and philosophy is certainly enough to explain why so many people have come away with the impression.

To understand ancient Greece (or Hellas, as the ancient Greeks themselves called it), think back to what was said about Sumer in an earlier chapter—namely that it was a cohesive empire in the sense that it was a practical assembly of city-states. In the same way, ancient Greece, during its golden age, wasn't so much an empire as it was a loose cluster of city-states, each achieving supremacy for a while.

THE ATHENS PERIOD

Athens is probably what you think of when you envision ancient Greece. The Parthenon, Socrates and Plato, most of the well-known works of Greek poetry and plays—all are the legacy of the city-state of Athens. Occupied off and on for the better part of five thousand years, Athens was a world of its own. But when educated Europeans rediscovered Greek political philosophy in the eighteenth century (as we'll discuss later) they began to see classical Athens as a peaceful utopia. In reality, however, it was neither peaceful nor particularly utopian.

It was, in fact, the military prowess of Athens that played a decisive role in preventing Greece from becoming just another part of the Persian Empire. Sparta was important to this process too—no question—but it was Athens that first defeated Persia at the Battle of Marathon in 490 B.C.E., and the Athenians continued to play a central military role for the remainder of the Greco-Persian Wars (499–449 B.C.E.). Classical Athens wasn't as militaristic as Sparta, but it was still fundamentally a military culture.

Athens did innovate new ways of governing that have taken hold over the past few centuries, but it wasn't fundamentally a utopia. Yes, the Athenians were technically the world's first democracy (and for nearly two centuries), but only wealthy male citizens over eighteen (about 15 percent of the population) were eligible to vote. And like most Greek city-states, they practiced slavery on a large scale—something that distinguished the Greeks from their Persian invaders, who had taken formal steps to abolish it.

That said, it's by and large a very good thing for those of us living today that the eighteenth-century political philosophers who rediscovered the traditions of Athens thought it was a more enlightened society than it was. Because these political philosophers thought they were restoring an old system of values rather than creating a new one, they didn't have to ask themselves whether democracy and human rights were possible. The shining example they saw in Athens—inaccurate as their assessment of it was—had given them their answer.

Praxis

Aristotle taught that human behavior falls into one of three categories: *theoria* (thinking), *poiesis* (creating), and *praxis* (doing). The word *praxis* has carried over to today's English to mean an intentional mode of action, distinguishable both from what we merely intend to do and from our subconscious habits. It's the root of such words as *practice* and *practical*.

HOW SPARTA UNITED THE PELOPONNESE

Anyone who has taken a high school world history course probably remembers hearing about the Peloponnesian War (431–404 B.C.E.), but there are some things about the Peloponnesian League, the winning coalition led by Sparta, that usually don't get as much attention as they should. To begin with, you might be wondering why people make such a big deal out of the whole Peloponnesian thing. Why not just call it the ancient Greek civil war or the Spartan war or something catchier like that? The Peloponnese is just a peninsula in southwestern Greece, and sure, that's where Sparta was, and sure, it was at the center of the conflict, and sure, it was called the Peloponnesian League because it united the city-states of that peninsula. But there's another very good reason why the Spartans placed so much emphasis on reminding people of the war's Peloponnesian character: tradition.

Think about where the culture of ancient Greece was in the fifth century B.C.E. Athens was the undisputed metropolis and intellectual capital of the region, it was wealthy with trade, and it was the site of the greatest political innovation. Sparta, in contrast, was a pretty ordinary monarchy, mandatory military service being its primary distinguishing feature. If you were running Sparta and you were trying to gather allies against Athens, you wouldn't be able to rely on a humanitarian argument or a financial argument or even the guarantee of victory. You'd have to work a lot harder than that.

The Olympics

Sparta had another ally in their quest to make the Peloponnese the center of Greek identity: the Olympics. Dating back at least as far as the eighth century B.C.E., the Olympics were effectively an international event, held every four years in the Peloponnese in the Olympia valley just outside of Elis, to honor both Zeus and his grandson Pelops. And these games didn't just draw huge crowds; they played a crucial role in linking the Greek city-states together and keeping them on friendly terms.

Sparta used its political and military muscle to overthrow local governments, protect its allies from mutual enemies, and otherwise dominate the peninsula. But among Sparta's greatest secret weapons was history. The Peloponnese was named after the legendary figure Pelops, grandson of Zeus, and the residents would have known that it was also home to Greece's oldest civilization, that of the Mycenae.

Although the Mycenae ruins were technically closer to Athens than Sparta, they were on the Peloponnese peninsula. By emphasizing that this was a war between the Peloponnese and island city-states, the Spartans were able to push forward the narrative that they were defending the Greek ancestral homeland from usurpers.

THE EMPIRE OF ALEXANDER THE GREAT

The World Is Not Enough

Sufficit huic tumulus, cui non suffecerit orbis. ("A tomb now suffices him for whom the world was not enough.")

—An epitaph, allegedly used for the (now lost) tomb of Alexander the Great (356–323 B.C.E.)

Ancient Greece long operated as a cluster of city-states like Sumer, but Philip II (382–336 B.C.E.) of Macedon not only put the region under imperial control, he made it impossible for loose confederations of city-states to ever operate safely in the region again. That seems like enough legacy for one bloodline, but compared to his son, Alexander the Great, whose empire stretched out across three continents, Phillip was an underachiever.

Over the course of this book we're going to talk a lot about globalism: the tendency countries have to make decisions based on international connections, rather than focusing on purely local or regional issues. Alexander basically invented globalism, and he did it by dominating, killing, and otherwise conquering more people than any human being ever had up to that point. The connections he indirectly created between the countries he invaded are still with us, in very different forms, to this day.

SPARTA, THEBES, AND MACEDON

The Peloponnesian War left Sparta as the dominant Greek city-state at the end of 404 B.C.E., but the thing about loose confederations of city-states is that it's hard for one power to stay in control for long. The leaders of Sparta soon learned what the leaders of Athens had discovered: that it's much harder to keep power than it is to acquire it. In 395 B.C.E., after less than a decade of power, Sparta faced a Persian-backed revolt from the cities of Thebes, Athens, Corinth, and Argos. The conflict, remembered by historians as the Corinthian War, would last for decades. Finally, at the Battle of Leuctra in 371 B.C.E., the Thebans crushed the Spartan army and laid to rest the idea of Spartan military supremacy. Although it remained autonomous for centuries to come, Sparta would never again dominate the region.

Thebes fared a little better, but only a little, and this is where the Macedonians move to the center of the story. By the late 330s B.C.E., Philip II of Macedon had already gathered an impressive number of Greek city-states under his control. Macedon decisively defeated the Theban army at the Battle of Chaeronea in 338 B.C.E., and by that point Greece was, by virtue of Philip's conquests, under Macedonian control. While it was still technically a confederation of city-states, most of Greece functioned, by virtue of Philip's military hierarchy, as a single empire. He chose to direct the full force of that empire against Greece's historic enemies, the Persians, who had themselves attempted to conquer Greece less than two centuries before.

But in 336 B.C.E., just as Philip attempted to gather public sentiment, funds, and supplies together to support an invasion against Persia, something unexpected happened: his own bodyguard murdered him. His office fell to his twenty-year-old son, Alexander III, a young man who had been taught that he was born to rule an empire. Specifically, Persia's empire.

Hellenization

Alexander's objective wasn't just to rule over a massive empire in his lifetime; it was to permanently make the world more Greek by spreading Greek language, religion, and cultural values. Since the people of Greece call their country Hellas, historians call this process Hellenization.

FATE AND CONQUEST

Philip's dream lived on in his son Alexander, which could have been merely cute but turned out to be something far more consequential and significantly bloodier. Alexander, who had been tutored by the Greek philosopher Aristotle (384–322 B.C.E.), had been taught that fate was primary to his life—that "everything that happens happens out of necessity," as Aristotle put it. For Alexander this idea of fate seems to have raised a possibility similar to the idea of the Mandate of Heaven (which is discussed later) and Manifest Destiny (also discussed later): that if you *can* rule the world, it means you're probably *supposed* to. Having inherited a massive army, a popular mandate, an impressive role model, a well-rounded civilian and military education, reasonable natural military aptitude, and an unfinished plan to invade Persia, Alexander came into power with his to-do list already in place.

The Road Runner to Alexander's Wile E. Coyote was the Persian king Darius III (ca. 380–330 B.C.E.), whose belief in destiny must have been shaken by that point. Darius III inherited his empire in his early forties and was only a few years younger than Alexander's father, Philip; whereas Alexander himself inherited his empire in his early twenties. What's worse, while Alexander grew up watching his beloved father and their beloved Macedon become more powerful by the day, Darius had just lived through decades of messy and soul-crushing palace intrigue and inherited a hobbled Achaemenid Empire that seemed to be falling apart even before Alexander invaded. The legacy of Cyrus the Great and the original Darius was a distant memory, and the unhappy leaders of Persia's provinces must have viewed it with a certain amount of skepticism. Darius III must have also been concerned about his job security; his predecessor, Artaxerxes IV, was definitely poisoned, and there are historical sources suggesting that his predecessor's predecessor, Artaxerxes III, may have been poisoned as well. Darius wasn't an optimist, and he didn't frighten easily; he was not initially concerned about the threat Alexander posed.

Besides, it looked at first as if Alexander might have plenty to deal with at home. After Philip's death, Thebes—which had preceded Macedon as the dominant Greek city-state—joined with other city-states to stage a revolt. Alexander responded by defeating and then destroying Thebes, and nobody challenged his authority after that. For most rulers uniting Greece so tightly under the leadership of one city-state would have been enough for one lifetime. Not so with Alexander, who quickly moved into Persian territory and began his conquest. One factor that made his victories especially achievable was that, by this point, many of Persia's provinces were going broke and were ready for new leadership. By the time he reached Egypt, for example, the local government didn't even put up a fight—they surrendered as soon as Alexander arrived, and they welcomed their new pharaoh as the physical incarnation of Osiris. By the end of 331 B.C.E., little remained of the Achaemenid Empire—but Alexander wasn't done. After the Battle of the Persian Gate in 330 B.C.E., he decisively defeated Darius's army, marched into Persepolis, and destroyed the Achaemenid Empire forever. In only six years, he had fully achieved Philip's ambition.

This isn't to say that Alexander necessarily hated the Persians; he just loved them in an intermittently murderous way. All three of his wives were Persian, for example, and his attitude toward Darius seemingly approached hero-worship. When Darius was later assassinated by his own cousin, Alexander's army captured the killer and tortured him to death. Historians credibly record that Darius's own mother and his lover-attendant became Alexander's companions after the Persian king's death, which could be attributed to their respect for the friendly rivalry between the two rulers or to Stockholm syndrome—take your pick.

In any case, Alexander just wasn't the same after the Achaemenid Empire fell. He spent seven years expanding the borders of Macedonia beyond the Persian boundaries, but as his conquests in India became increasingly difficult, the morale of his men began to understandably decrease. When Alexander's exhausted army reached the Ganges, with a massive and well-equipped army waiting to potentially slaughter them on the other side, Alexander's men pled with him to let them go back home. He complied, and then he wept.

Folk history tells us that Alexander cried because he had no more worlds to conquer. But that was never entirely true, as the Mongolians would later prove by conquering over four times as much territory on the same continents. Maybe he cried because he felt there were no more worlds to conquer *for him*. If Alexander's army had kept marching past the point of exhaustion and attrition, they would have eventually been defeated, if not slaughtered outright, and this period of history would have become a cautionary tale about Alexander the Doomed instead of a legend about Alexander the Great. The outcome for Alexander would have been, in any case, the same; while dreaming of new military campaigns, he died under mysterious circumstances in Babylon.

Roxana of Bactria

All three of Alexander's wives—Roxana, Stateira, and Parysatis—were born in Persia. Of the three, Roxana is by far the most famous, and she is the only one who produced an heir. Roxana's story as recorded by historians is the stuff of Greek tragedy: she's said to have assassinated both Stateira and Parysatis after Alexander's death, so as to secure her son's claim to kingship, but was herself assassinated (along with her son, Alexander IV) shortly before he was to inherit the throne at fourteen.

THE FIRST EMPEROR OF QIN

The Power of a United China

"The straightening board was created because of warped wood, and the plumb line came into being because of things that are not straight. Rulers are established, and ritual and rightness are illuminated, because human nature is evil."
—Xunzi (ca. 300–230 B.C.E.), Chinese philosopher

Today, China is the most populous country on Earth and is the fourth largest in terms of land mass. With 297 living languages and fifty-six recognized ethnic groups, China's incredible size, diversity, and influence makes it sometimes seem more like a continent than a nation. This was no less true in ancient times than it is today, which raises a difficult question: how did China end up as a single country in the first place?

Can the Great Wall of China Be Seen from the Moon?

It's often said that the Great Wall of China is the only man-made object that's visible from the moon with the naked eye. In reality, no man-made structure falls into that category. Portions of the Great Wall can be seen from the International Space Station, but only if you're lucky and know exactly where to look.

For the first half of its 5,000-year history, China was more of a region—like the Middle East—than a country. Ancient nations called it the Middle Kingdom, so named because they believed that it lay at the center of the world's map. But it wasn't just one kingdom until the Qin state conquered all of China at the end of the Warring States Period (475–221 B.C.E.), briefly bringing it under centralized control and setting a precedent that future pan-Chinese nations would follow.

THE WISDOM OF CONFUCIUS

Although ancient Chinese philosophy is as rich and complex as that of the Greeks, it has not received a comparable level of attention in the West. One philosopher whose work has been studied with some seriousness by Western scholars is Confucius (551–479 B.C.E), who taught that we can best serve the world by refining our consciences and developing virtues, not by attempting to reason out and live by specific universal rules of conduct.

Central to Confucius's philosophy is the idea that we're all of more-or-less equal value at birth but can develop good or bad traits over the course of our lives by cultivating specific habits. This is an idea that we take for granted now, but for most of human history in the West it was pretty radical. Emperors who believed that they and their families were destined from birth to rule found it particularly problematic.

At the end of the Warring States Period, the founding Qin emperor Qin Shi Huang (ca. 259–210 B.C.E.) banned Confucianism, attempted to burn its texts, and slaughtered its supporters—but this attempt to suppress the religion ultimately failed. When the Han dynasty took control in 202 B.C.E., they had a more tolerant attitude toward the religion. By the time of the Three Kingdoms period in the third century, Confucianism had become the most influential philosophical system in China.

The Art of War

Although the legendary general Sun Tzu is traditionally said to have lived even earlier in China's history, most leading contemporary historians now say that he lived during the Warring States Period. His *The Art of War*, which has been used as a strategy guide both on and off the battlefield for thousands of years, is still refreshingly honest and pragmatic. Among the advice he offers:

- "All warfare is based on deception. Hence when we are able to attack, we must seem unable; when using our forces, we must seem inactive; when we are near, we must make the enemy believe we are far away; when far away, we must make him believe we are near. Hold out baits to entice the enemy, feign disorder, and crush him."
- "There is no instance of a country having benefited from prolonged warfare."
- "Supreme excellence consists in breaking the enemy's resistance without fighting."
- "When you surround an army, leave an outlet free. Do not press a desperate foe too hard."
- "There are five dangerous faults which may affect a general: (1) recklessness, which leads to destruction; (2) cowardice, which leads to capture; (3) a hasty temper, which can be provoked by insults; (4) a delicacy of honor, which is sensitive to shame; (5) over-solicitude for his men, which exposes him to worry and trouble."

THE REIGN OF THE EMPEROR ASHOKA

Pillars of the Remorseful King

"Beloved-of-the-Gods, King [Ashoka], conquered the Kalingas eight years after his coronation. 150,000 were deported, 100,000 were killed, and many more died for other reasons. After the Kalingas had been conquered, Beloved-of-the-Gods came to feel a strong inclination towards the Buddha's teachings, a love for the Buddha's teachings and for instruction in the Buddha's teachings. Now Beloved-of-the-Gods feels deep remorse for having conquered the Kalingas."

—From the edicts of the emperor Ashoka (ca. 304–232 B.C.E.)

Ashoka is the only figure in history to be universally revered as one of the world's most brutally effective conquerors *and* a pacifistic Buddhist saint. But, as you might have guessed, he didn't try to wear both hats at the same time. Ashoka was the third emperor of the Maurya Empire. When he took power in 268 B.C.E. the Mauryas already controlled most of India plus a sizeable chunk of the area we now call Afghanistan. But he had a problem with Kalinga, a large tough-as-nails holdout nation on the eastern coast of the Indian peninsula, and he made conquering this region his first priority. He succeeded, at great human cost, but he felt really bad about it. Like a lot of other people throughout history who felt really bad about things, Ashoka got religion.

In this case the religion was Buddhism—pacifist, vegetarian, antimaterialist Buddhism—and it raised a few really tough questions that nobody had ever had to answer before: How should a Buddhist emperor govern? How can you renounce material wealth when you control a two-million-square-mile empire? How can you renounce violence when you're in charge of one of the largest armies that, up to that point, had ever existed? Ashoka answered those questions in a way that would change the world forever.

ALL APOLOGIES

Buddhism has had a major role in reshaping most of the major Asian powers, but India—the homeland of the Buddha himself—was the first. At the time Ashoka took power, Buddhism was a fairly young religion and had not yet spread to China, where the traditions of Zen and Tibetan Buddhism originated, nor had Mahayana or Theravada Buddhism, the Buddhist traditions that would later prove most popular within India, been founded.

At this point in history, Buddhism was still a relatively small movement and effectively pre-denominational. The Buddha himself is said to have lived only two or three centuries before Ashoka. So the decision Ashoka made to adopt Buddhism would have been seen as eccentric, comparable to the decision Pharaoh Akhenaten made to downplay polytheism in ancient Egypt or the Roman emperor Constantine's later decision to convert to Christianity. But when you've inherited control over the dominant empire in the region, and you've already mounted a successful military campaign against its last remaining serious adversary, you're in a unique position to make religious innovations. Ashoka did this, contributing as much to the spread of Buddhism as Buddhism did to the trajectory of his reign.

That's saying a lot, because it's difficult to overstate the degree to which Buddhism really did change Ashoka's trajectory. To start with, Ashoka wasn't just remorseful on his own behalf; he was also implicitly remorseful on behalf of his late father, the emperor Bindusara (ca. 320–273 B.C.E.), who had dramatically expanded the Maurya Empire but failed to conquer the Kalingas. For Ashoka to carry his father's program forward, and then govern based on the idea that what he and his father had accomplished was evil, had never happened before in the history of empires and would never happen again.

The Four Noble Truths

The most fundamental tenet of Buddhism is that life is suffering. This is the first of the Four Noble Truths, which state in turn that this pain is caused by desire, that it is possible to learn to let go of desire, and that there is a system of behavior—called the Eightfold Path—that, if followed consistently, will inevitably teach you to do so.

WHEN SORRY ISN'T ENOUGH

While many emperors distributed monuments intended to make themselves sound better then they actually were, Ashoka had his apologies engraved on dozens of fifty-foot sandstone pillars and distributed them throughout his empire (nineteen still survive). But Ashoka wasn't just trying to make amends—the pillars also included Ashoka's promises on behalf of local rulers to respect basic human rights, making the Ashokan pillars among the world's earliest binding human rights documents. Later, scribes would engrave records of future events on these pillars, providing a permanent history of their time.

THE RISE OF THE ROMAN REPUBLIC

The City on the Hills

"Let arms yield to togas, and laurels to speeches."

—Cicero (106–43 B.C.E.)

Some two thousand years ago, legend had it that the first Roman king Romulus founded the city on April 21, 753 B.C.E. And for much of its early history, Rome doesn't appear to have been that terribly different from the Mediterranean city-states that surrounded it. Then, in or by 509 B.C.E., the Roman people did something unique: they overthrew their king and established the Roman Republic.

The new republic initially expanded by gradually defeating ancient civilizations in the region. These civilizations were made obscure by these defeats—so obscure that most of us have never heard of them: the Latin League in 496 B.C.E., the Volsci in 338 B.C.E., the Hernici in 306 B.C.E., and so on. By 200 B.C.E., Rome was a dominant power in the region. And by 100 B.C.E., with territory stretching across both the southern coast of Europe and the northern coast of Africa, the Roman Republic had become a dominant power in the world.

HOW THE WEST WAS WON

For historians of the West, the Roman Republic bridges the gap between the relatively mysterious ancient civilizations that preceded it and the more familiar political systems that would follow. Like other ancient civilizations, the Roman civilization had a polytheistic religion that celebrated figures who existed before written history did; it originated as a loose confederation of independent city-states; and it was really, really old. But like a more contemporary civilization, it was a republic—that is, it had a relatively modern, representative, bureaucratic kind of government. And, actually, the Roman Republic gave the West most of the political vocabulary it still uses today.

Aeneas

Roman storytellers were heavily influenced by Greek culture, and they looked for ways to ground the story of their republic in ancient Greek folklore. They found a point of connection in Aeneas, a mythical Trojan War hero described in Homer's *The Iliad*, whom the Romans decided was an ancestor of Romulus. The poet Virgil (70–19 B.C.E.) made Aeneas the hero of his own epic poem, *The Aeneid*, and he quickly became a national symbol of patriotism and traditional Roman values.

CARTHAGO DELENDA EST (CARTHAGE MUST BE DESTROYED)

Rome is the Eternal City, the capital of the West, the former seat of the Roman Empire. But it almost wasn't any of those things, and it may be difficult for modern readers to appreciate just how close an abandoned city on the northern coast of Africa came to becoming the capital of the Western world. The Carthaginians, who lived in what we now call Tunisia, were a dominant military and trade power who butted heads with the Greeks *and* the Romans over the course of four centuries, and proved to be worthy adversaries to both.

Much of the dispute between Carthage and Rome had to do with land, specifically the island of Sicily. After a series of skirmishes involving Sicilian mercenaries that left Carthage with control over the Strait of Messina, the two-mile-wide naval passageway between Sicily and the Italian peninsula, Rome found itself potentially blockaded by a major military power. The Romans preemptively attacked, and a series of three wars—which historians call the Punic Wars—resulted.

What Does *Punic* Mean?

The founders of Carthage were Phoenicians, from an area along the coast of the eastern Mediterranean. The word *Punic* comes from Phoenicia, so the wars between Rome and Carthage came to be called the Punic Wars.

The most famous of these wars, and the deadliest to Rome, was the Second Punic War, which put much of Italy briefly under the control of the Carthaginian general Hannibal Barca (ca. 247–183 B.C.E.). In 218 B.C.E., ten years after the Romans killed his father Hamilcar, and three years after they killed his brother Hasdrubal, Hannibal undertook a strategy that the Romans did not expect and could not have prepared for: a land invasion from the north. Describing the 986-mile journey as "arduous" doesn't do it justice; it involved marching through hundreds of miles of hostile foreign territory and getting a massive army across the Alps into Italy, something that would have been viewed by most people with good sense as physically impossible. But the prospect of defeating Rome forever, and avenging his family, must have been a powerful motivator. And he almost did both, running roughshod over the Italian peninsula, conquering cities, drawing supporters, and disrupting the business of the Roman Republic for fifteen years before his army finally left for Carthage in 203 B.C.E.

Ultimately the Romans went on to defeat and then conquer Carthage. But what's interesting is how close Carthage came to victory. The Romans never stopped fearing Carthage in general, or Hannibal in particular. Decades later, when he was on his deathbed, Hannibal is said to have written in a letter: "Let us relieve the Romans from the anxiety they have so long experienced, since they think it tries their patience too much to wait for an old man's death."

Cato the Elder (234–149 B.C.E.)

Marcus Porcius Cato was, in effect, the John McCain of the Roman Republic: a war hero, a champion of ancestral tradition, a thorn in the side of whoever the executive happened to be at the time, and a lovable curmudgeon. His great-grandson Cato the Younger (95–46 B.C.E.) became nearly as widely known among historians for his rebellion against Julius Caesar, but they called the elder Cato "Cato Priscus"—"Cato the Ancient"—a good half-century before the kid was even born.

ROME BECOMES AN EMPIRE

Marble and Blood

"I found Rome a city of bricks, and I left it a city a marble."

—Augustus (63 B.C.E.–C.E. 14), as quoted by Suetonius

Want to get rid of entrenched bureaucracy and put everything under the control of a proven leader who can get things done? The Romans of the first century B.C.E. certainly did, and so they destroyed their 460-year-old republic. In its place, after briefly flirting with a dictator, they installed an emperor.

Things did quickly get better for the Roman Empire thanks to four decades of competent dictatorship under the emperor Augustus, who happened to be the previous dictator's great nephew. But let's be honest: that's not an outcome anyone could have predicted at the time. The Roman Empire got lucky—so lucky that, two thousand years later, the Western world is *still* to a great extent Roman in its political priorities.

FROM GENERAL TO DICTATOR

There was no single figure more important in the history of the Roman Republic *or* the Roman Empire than Gaius Julius Caesar (100–44 B.C.E.), who killed the former and gave birth to the latter. A scandal-ridden governor and military hero who had successfully led the Roman army to a series of victories over the Gauls (a coalition of tribes in what we now call France), Caesar marched home in 49 B.C.E., violated Roman law, and promptly took command of the government as dictator. But he had his reasons, and the biggest reason was a rivalry with Pompey the Great (106–48 B.C.E.), a general popular with the Roman Senate (note: Caesar was not) with decades of military conquests behind him.

Crossing the Rubicon

When Julius Caesar ordered his army across the river Rubicon back into Roman territory without surrendering his military authority over to civilians, he violated the sacred traditions of the Roman Republic and instantly branded himself a traitor in the eyes of the law. To this day, people say someone has "crossed the Rubicon" when she or he has made a risky but irreversible decision.

The Roman Republic of the first century B.C.E. was all about three great generals: Caesar, Pompey, and a guy named Marcus Linius Crassus (115–53 B.C.E.). The three shared power and loot within the relatively weak and corrupt Roman Republic under an agreement that historians would later call the First Triumvirate—literally, the government "of three men" (Latin: *trium virorum*). But after Crassus kicked the bucket at the hands of the Parthians (in what we'd now call Syria), Pompey took advantage of Caesar's apparent political naïveté and his time away from Rome to claim power all for himself. Unfortunately for Pompey, Caesar was both more popular and more audacious than Pompey had imagined. By early 44 B.C.E., the Roman Republic had become a dictatorship under Caesar, though Caesar had not claimed the title of emperor. He had to die before people would call him that.

And die he did. On March 15, 44 B.C.E., he was stabbed twenty-three times by a crowd of assassins that included the young senators Marcus Junius Brutus (85–42 B.C.E.) and Gaius Cassius Longinus (also 85–42 B.C.E.). They thought that in killing Caesar they'd restored the Roman Republic. As it turns out, they'd doomed it.

CLEOPATRA, THE SECOND TRIUMVIRATE, AND THE SECOND CAESAR

Both Pompey and the young Roman senators had underestimated Caesar's popularity, but a dead dictator isn't much of a dictator, no matter how popular he is. What the people of Rome did decide was that this republic business needed to end. The Roman Senate had long been criticized as a plaything of the idle rich, and the one thing it had going for it was that it wasn't the kind of government where stabbing people was a viable political strategy. The death of the surprisingly beloved dictator Caesar meant the death of the Senate, and the rise of a more formal Second Triumvirate made up of three of Caesar's allies: the charismatic populist Mark Antony (83–30 B.C.E.), the high priest Marcus Aemilius Lepidus (89–13 B.C.E.), and Caesar's own twenty-year-old nephew Gaius Octavius (63 B.C.E.–C.E. 19), also known as Octavian. Unlike the First Triumvirate, these three men weren't just treated as if they ruled the country—they were literally granted emergency powers to rule the country.

Like Caesar and Pompey, they were also military commanders—charged with suppressing armies that Brutus and Longinus had raised in hopes of reconquering Rome and bringing back the republic. The Second Triumvirate did this decisively in October 42 B.C.E. at the Battle of Philippi, in a victory so complete that both Brutus and Longinus committed suicide rather than attempt to negotiate terms of surrender. In an eerie reversal of the First Triumvirate's fate, Mark Antony took on control of Gaul, the eastern provinces, and engaged a popular war with those deadly Crassus-slaying Parthians. Meanwhile, Octavian began to consolidate his authority in Rome. Lepidus, who was assigned North Africa, largely fades from the story at this point.

Like Pompey, Octavian clearly felt that he should rule Rome alone. Unlike Pompey, he didn't overplay his hand. Like Caesar, Antony focused on securing power abroad. Unlike Caesar, he didn't have a deteriorating Roman Republic to rebel against. But Antony had one thing that Octavian didn't: a powerful ally in the Egyptian ruler Cleopatra VII Philopator (69–30 B.C.E.), who was every bit Octavian's match in political cunning. She was also the mother of Caesar's only known surviving biological son, Ptolemy Caesar (47–30 B.C.E.), a.k.a. Little Caesar (which is where the pizza chain got its name), who had already been recognized as such by the Roman government. This alone posed a practical challenge to Octavian, whose legitimacy was based in part on his status as Caesar's nephew and adopted son. If that wasn't enough, Rome depended on Egypt's grain for survival.

Antony and Cleopatra became collaborators, lovers, and—potentially—future rulers of the emerging Roman Empire. This is the way things remained for nine years, and if they had gone on that way for another nine the history of the Western world might have been very different. Upon coming of age, Little Caesar, who was descended both from the Egyptian Ptolemaic dynasty and Julius Caesar, would have been ideally positioned to claim his father's legacy. Time was not on Octavian's side.

Senate

The Roman Senate wasn't just a chamber of the legislature; it reflected the privileged status ancient societies generally gave to the old in reverence to their wisdom. The Latin word from which senate is derived, *senex*, refers to a person who is elderly. It is the same word from which *senior* is derived. In terms of the word's original meaning, a senate is literally a council of elders.

Fortunately for Octavian, Mark Antony made one fatal blunder: he married Cleopatra in 32 B.C.E., making himself a bigamist (as he had already married Octavian's sister in 40 B.C.E.). This gave Octavian a pretense to obtain Antony's will, and what he found there doomed the Second Triumvirate: a promise to leave Rome's eastern provinces in the hands of Cleopatra and Caesarion (Little Caesar) upon his death, and a request to be buried in Alexandria rather than Rome. The Roman Senate authorized a declaration of war against Cleopatra. Antony sided with her, and the final war of the Roman Republic commenced. In a little more than two years, it was over—Antony and Cleopatra committed suicide in a besieged Alexandria, and Caesarion was executed at the hands of Octavian's forces. In 27 B.C.E., Octavian took on the name Caesar Augustus and became the first emperor of Rome, though he considered himself the second—Julius Caesar, who claimed the power but not the title, being the first.

JESUS CHRIST AND HIS TIMES

The Rebel on the Cross

"To get rid of the report [that he had set the Roman fire himself], Nero fastened the guilt and inflicted the most exquisite tortures on a class hated for their abominations, called Christians by the populace. Christus, from whom the name had its origin, suffered the extreme penalty during the reign of Tiberius at the hands of one of our procurators, Pontius Pilatus..."

—The Roman historian Tacitus (c.e. 56–120)

For most of ancient history a ruler was also identified as a god. This was made explicit in the case of ancient Egypt, where the pharaoh was expected to act as an intermediary between gods and humans, but it was more or less implicit in most other nations as well. This isn't just a primitive belief—if earthly power isn't proof that somebody up there likes you, what is? Indeed, contemporary religious folk who buy into the idea that God rewards his most beloved followers with material goods are carrying that idea forward into the current age.

This philosophy has its share of detractors. One of them is reported to have said that it is better to be meek, poor in spirit, to hunger and thirst for righteousness (Matthew 5:3), that it's really, really hard for a rich man to win God's favor at all (Matthew 19:24), and that people who make violence their business will eventually become violence's business (Matthew 26:52). Jesus, the person to whom these remarks are attributed, would ultimately become the most powerful man on Earth, but he had to die first. He was one of many people who was given the title of messiah, only to be executed on a Roman cross.

THE MESSIAH'S BURDEN

The story of Jesus as we've received it actually begins with the letters of St. Paul of Tarsus (ca. 5–67), who began as a zealous member of the Jewish faith before converting to Christianity and committing himself to spreading the new religion throughout the Roman Empire. It's Paul's letters—and especially his epistles to the growing Christian communities in Rome, Corinth, Galatia, Ephesus, Philippi, Collossae, and Thessaloniki—that make up the bulk of the New Testament outside of the Gospels. Their historicity isn't in question; they're both the earliest and most candid Christian documents. What they tell us about the ancient world in general, and the oppressive power of the Roman Empire in particular, is striking.

As you may remember from an earlier chapter, in all likelihood we owe the existence of the Hebrew Bible to the oppression of the Babylonians, who forced early Jewish communities to write down their oral histories before they were lost. These communities anxiously awaited a messiah, or rescuer, whom they identified with the Persian emperor Cyrus the Great (ca. 600–530 B.C.E.). This isn't historical speculation; Isaiah 45 specifically calls Cyrus the messiah and identifies him as the divinely-anointed savior of the Jewish people. And their trust in Cyrus was well-founded. Unlike the Babylonians, who based their political system on their national religion and saw other religions as a threat to national security, the Persian rulers were Zoroastrians—members of a religion that did not treat other religions as a political threat—and treated members of minority faiths, such as Judaism, with respect.

An Eyewitness Account

Outside of the New Testament, the earliest records of the Christian movement come from the Jewish historian Flavius Josephus (ca. 37–100), whose *The Antiquities of the Jews*—written no later than C.E. 94—include references to Jesus, his brother James, and John the Baptist. Although it's impossible to know for certain what he originally said about Jesus—existing manuscripts show that the paragraph referring to Jesus, called the Testimonium Flavium by theologians, appears to have been edited—the fact that he *did* mention Jesus, to whom he refers later in the text, is not in dispute. Neither is his reference to the death of John the Baptist, which he treats as a major event of significant historical importance.

ROME AND BABYLON

During the first century C.E. what we now call Israel and Palestine was called Judaea. It was a province of the Roman Empire, and the citizens of Judaea saw significant parallels to the Babylonian Empire. Referring to Rome as Babylon, as was done in 1 Peter 5:13, was a common practice. The Romans weren't as consistently oppressive as the Babylonians, but there were some oppressive traits in common. For one thing, Roman civic religion—like Babylonian religion—treated foreign religions, such as Judaism (and, later, Christianity), with suspicion. For another, the Roman Empire had an unfortunate habit of intentionally offending the religious sensibilities of the Judaean population, then violently quashing any protests that resulted from it. This made the Jewish search for a new messiah, a Cyrus the Great for their age, a dangerous endeavor. One particularly cruel method of execution, crucifixion, involved stripping someone naked, nailing or binding them to a wooden cross, displaying them in front of their own communities as they died in agony, and then (quite often) letting their bodies publicly rot. The Romans considered it to be an effective deterrent to would-be messiahs, a final rebuttal to the idea that someone was anointed by God to be a savior.

So when Jesus was crucified and followers spread the belief that he had returned from the dead after three days, it destroyed the effectiveness of his crucifixion. Records of the early Christian church even suggest that early Christians intentionally sought out crucifixion as a way of uniting with Jesus. It is no small thing that Christianity, a religion that was founded in the wake of the Roman Empire's execution of a revolutionary figure, would, within a matter of several centuries, itself become the official religion of the Roman Empire.

The Holy Grail

One European Christian tradition holds that the cup from which Jesus drank at the Last Supper, which was also purportedly used to catch a few drops of his blood during the Crucifixion, still survives and grants magical powers to whoever uses it. Although this seems unlikely from a historian's point of view—no references to a Christian Holy Grail predate the late twelfth century—the legend of the Grail was popular in medieval Europe and continues to capture the public imagination, playing a central role in films such as *Indiana Jones and the Last Crusade* (1989) and *The Da Vinci Code* (2006).

CHINA'S SIX DYNASTIES PERIOD

A Fragmented Empire

"Make a sound in the east, then strike in the west."
—From the thirty-six military strategies of Tan Daoji (d. 436)

One of the things Westerners tend to forget about the major Asian powers of China, India, and Japan is that they're extremely diverse and difficult to unite. This is especially true of China, which is more than twice the size of India and Japan combined. Add in the fact that countries in general are prone to splitting up and having civil wars from time to time, and it's no surprise that the unity China achieved under the Qin and Han dynasties wasn't permanent.

When the Han dynasty collapsed in 220 after four centuries of relatively peaceful rule, an era of Three Kingdoms emerged in its place...then sixteen kingdoms, then two, then one. Chinese historians remember this period as the Six Dynasties period—so named because it was a period during which the Chinese government burned through six different dynasties in only 369 years, for an average of sixty-one and a half years per dynasty. It was a time of constant change and instability, where people could plausibly live long enough to see two major shifts in power during a single lifetime.

The Three Kingdoms (220–280)

China's original Three Kingdoms were:

- The Shu Kingdom, the first of the three to fall to the emerging Jin dynasty in 263.
- The Wei Kingdom from which the Jin dynasty emerged, which collapsed in 265.
- The massive Eastern Wu Kingdom, which controlled China's coast and most of the inland territory. Its fall in 280 at the hands of the Jin marked the end of the Three Kingdoms period.

The Jin dynasty united China under a single emperor, which sounds like the beginning of a period of relative Chinese stability. But remember, this was the Six Dynasties period, and the Jin was only the second dynasty. Things were about to get messy.

The Sixteen Kingdoms (304–420)

In 304, after less than a quarter-century of Jin rule, corruption and a crisis over succession created an opening for ethnic coalitions in northern China to claim autonomy. The resulting period, called the Sixteen Kingdoms period, saw the Jin dynasty retreat to the eastern coast as small rival kingdoms quickly rose and fell.

Cao Cao (155–220)

Most people who become emperors do so during their own lifetimes, but the northern Chinese general Cao Cao holds the unusual distinction of becoming an ex-emperor without having ever become an emperor. It was his son, Cao Pi, who established the state of Cao Wei seven months after his father's death—and, just as Augustus had done in Rome, declared his father, not himself, to have been its founding emperor.

The Northern and Southern Dynasties (420–589)

By 420 the Wei dynasty had taken control of the north while the Liu Song dynasty had taken control of the south. China remained divided until the Sui dynasty took control of the country in 589, ending the Six Dynasties period and beginning a period of unity that would last for centuries.

THE PAX ROMANA AND BEYOND

The Age of Emperors

"The plunderers of the world, they have laid waste to the land till there is no more left, and now they scour the sea. If a people are rich they are worth robbing, if poor they are worth enslaving; and not the East nor the West can content their greedy maw. They are the only men in all the world whose lust of conquest makes them find in wealth and in poverty equally tempting baits. To robbery, murder, and outrage they give the lying name of government, and where they make a desert they call it peace."

—The native Scottish rebel Galgacus, speaking of the Romans, as quoted by the Roman historian Tacitus (56–120)

There are a lot of theories about why Rome fell, as if it were some abnormal event for a major empire to fall and not an inevitability, and that in itself is testament to the unique place the Roman Empire has in our understanding of world history. It would be just as reasonable to ask why it didn't fall sooner. How did it survive so many changes—growing and shrinking in size, transitioning from the old Roman pantheon to Christianity, violently absorbing often-unwilling societies with the expectation that these societies would be influenced, but would not influence them in return?

Technically speaking Rome fell twice: the original Western Roman Empire fell in 476 when Odoacer (433–493) became the first king of Italy, and the Eastern Roman Empire, which we later called

the Byzantine Empire, fell in 1453 when Constantinople was conquered by the Ottomans.

ROMAN PEACE AND ROMAN WAR

The Roman Empire established by Caesar Augustus in 27 B.C.E.
would last for almost exactly five hundred years. The first 206 years
were called the Pax Romana ("Roman peace") and were looked on
as a period of relative peace and prosperity, but it was peace only in
the narrowest sense. Constant border expansion, mass slaughter of
dissidents, disputes over the transfer of power, multiple assassina-
tions of emperors, and widespread corruption marked this period
in Roman history, just as it did any other. In fact the Pax Romana
included the reigns of both Caligula (12–41) and Nero (37–68), the
two most infamous emperors in Roman history. The difference is
that none of these factors actually interfered with the stability of the
government or its power over core territories.

Given that fact, you'd think that an event that occurred in 180
was something terrible and apocalyptic, something that tainted
the future of the Roman Empire forever, but it was something much
quieter than that: an ordinary succession. The beloved emperor and
Stoic philosopher Marcus Aurelius (121–180) died of smallpox at the
untimely but not shocking age of fifty-eight, and his son, the well-
prepared but volatile Lucius Aurelius Commodus (161–192), took
over. Commodus was hated by his contemporaries, and that hatred
has remained so strong through the centuries that the Emperor Commodus was the villain in the 2000 Russell Crowe flick *Gladiator*, but
his predecessors weren't angels and his successors weren't monsters.
In 192, he was assassinated—the first emperor in almost a century

to meet this fate, as far as history can tell us—and five prospective emperors battled it out until Septimius Severus (145–211) ended up in charge. He and his descendants ruled until the Imperial Crisis of 235–284, when the Roman Empire temporarily split into three warring states. The reforms of the emperor Diocletian (244–312) stabilized and reunited the empire. It split into warring factions again when Diocletian abdicated for health reasons in 305, but was united again by Constantine the Great (272–337) in 324. Upon his death, the Roman Empire experienced yet another civil war as his sons fought over control. (Constantine's decision to build Constantinople as a second capital of the Eastern Roman Empire had a more durable effect on history, as did his conversion to Christianity.)

Nero Didn't Fiddle While Rome Burned

Conventional wisdom says that during the catastrophic Roman fire of 64, which he would later blame on the Christians, the Emperor Nero fiddled. No records from the time suggest that he did, but the historians Suetonius and Tacitus relay reports that he *sang* a mournful song about the fall of Troy while he watched the fire. (Suetonius believed the story, while Tacitus was more skeptical.) Centuries later, historians expanded on this story and claimed that he was playing a musical instrument while he sang—but even if that were true (and we have no reason to believe it was), the fiddle hadn't been invented yet during Nero's lifetime.

In other words, when people refer to the Pax Romana, they're referring to a period in the Roman Empire's history when actual civil war wasn't on the radar. That's all the term means. The years during the Pax Romana weren't consistently great, and the years after weren't consistently terrible, but for 206 years the Roman Empire wasn't technically at war with itself. By the standards of the time, that was peace.

SO WHY DID ROME FALL?

In his six-volume masterpiece *The History of the Decline and Fall of the Roman Empire* (1788) the English historian Edward Gibbon (1737–1794) attributed the fall of the Roman Empire to "the triumph of barbarism and religion." I'm not going to say Gibbon was wrong, because he documented literally thousands of smaller events that contributed to the collapse of the Roman Empire. But we can nonetheless look at the question with fresh eyes.

Five Reasons Rome Might Have Fallen

1. **It was too big.** Aristotle famously wrote in his *Politics* that the city is the appropriate scale of government, and from a stability perspective that seems to be true. The oldest country on Earth according to most measures is the tiny (pop. 33,000) southern European nation of San Marino, which was founded in 301. For various reasons too obscure to go into here some historians disqualify San Marino, giving the oldest-nation nod to Iceland (pop. 332,000) or the Isle of Man (pop. 84,000). Meanwhile, the largest country that has ever existed—the Union of Soviet Socialist Republics (USSR)—lasted only sixty-nine years, and the most populous country that has ever existed, China, had *two* revolutions in the twentieth century (in 1912 and 1949). Keeping Europe under one umbrella is difficult under the best

of circumstances today, as advocates for the European Union have discovered. Taking all of these precedents into account, the fact that the Western Roman Empire survived for as long as it did is incredible.

2. **It was too inefficient.** There's a reason the ancient Chinese philosopher Confucius admired bureaucrats: in any large, centralized government, good bureaucrats are a must. The fact that the phrase *good bureaucrats* sounds like an oxymoron illustrates just how rare it is to live under a well-managed bureaucracy even now, what with our synchronized electronic databases and instantly searchable policy manuals. For anyone to be an effective bureaucrat in the age before that level of technology was available required near-superhuman talent from a large number of people, and that talent wasn't available.

3. **It was too poor.** The constant military conflict, infrastructure repair, and food distribution issues involved in administering the Roman Empire wore out its material resources. And when there were no more foreign palaces to raid, the empire could not sustain itself.

4. **It was too cruel.** The Western Roman Empire of its last few centuries had an unfortunate habit of hiring and training ethnic-minority "barbarians" to serve as legionaries (where they ultimately made up a majority). These troops murderously abused their kin to suppress revolts, and then fought them after they understandably defected to the other side. This pattern of behavior was foolish and self-destructive enough that it could have easily destroyed Rome on its own.

5. **People were simply tired of it.** When you face the previous problems and your people have no memory of what it was like to live in anything *but* the province of a slowly dying empire,

for generations upon generations, the temptation to try something new must have been overwhelming.

Patricians, Plebeians, Proletariat, and Slaves

Western societies still observe class distinctions between the wealthy, the middle class, and the working class, but in ancient Roman society the distinction was acknowledged and formalized. Patricians were Roman citizens descended from the *first* Romans, whereas plebeians ("plebes") were Roman citizens who came along later but gradually achieved equal status. The proletariat was made up of plebeians who were too poor to vote, and slaves weren't citizens at all.

INDIA UNDER THE GUPTAS

The Great Chessmasters

"There was Samudragupta, equal to the gods Dhanada and Antaka in pleasure and anger...by whom the whole tribe of kings upon the Earth was overtaken by loss of wealth and sovereignty."
—From inscriptions found in the abandoned city of Eran in northern India

Much of the timeline of ancient India is a mystery to the contemporary world, not because so few people kept written records but because so many did. Ancient India was one of the most literate societies on Earth at the time, and produced works of unparalleled scope and complexity. The *Mahabharata*, the national historical epic of India, is 1.8 million words long; by comparison, the entire Protestant Bible, containing both the Hebrew Bible and the New Testament, is about 775,000 words. And for all of its detail and complexity, the *Mahabharata* is only one version of the story among many, and it covers only a tiny fraction of the written history of the region.

Since there's no simple way to tell the story of ancient India, our popular understanding of this 5,000-year-old civilization tends to be based on the idea that, for most of its history, it was more or less permanently the nation of the Gupta Period: deeply religious and literary, with a wide range of well-established religious traditions. India of the Guptas is not the ancient India that always was, but it was the ancient India we tend to imagine.

Great Figures of the Gupta Period

- **Aryabhata (ca. 476–550),** the astronomer and mathematician who discovered several key elements necessary to the development of trigonometry.
- **Kalidasa (ca. 375–425),** the poet and playwright whose *Abhijñānaśākuntalam* is one of the most widely translated works of Sanskrit literature.
- **Vasubandhu (ca. 316–396),** a Buddhist philosopher who would help to establish the Mahayana school that would become the prevailing tradition in India and go on to influence Tibetan and Zen Buddhism.

Chaturanga

Indians of the Gupta Period invented the board game that we now call chess, but the rules of this game—which the Guptas would have called *chaturanga*, Sanskrit for "four limbs"—have changed dramatically over time. The term *four limbs* refers to the four divisions of the Indian army, each of which corresponded to a type of chess piece: the infantry (pawns), horse cavalry (knights), elephant cavalry (bishops), and chariots (rooks).

THE GOLDEN AGE OF THE MAYANS

The Long Count

"There are those who do not see your road."

—Mayan proverb

When you're talking about ancient Mesoamerican empires, you're usually talking more about communities that created and linked city-states than you are about empires in a traditional sense. In a previous chapter we spoke about the ancient Olmecs, but in terms of evidence of physical settlement Mayan civilization technically predates that of the Olmecs by about 1,500 years, rivaling Sumer and Egypt in age. And we talk about the Aztec interaction with colonial invaders, but the Mayans were still around as a civilization at that point too.

We'd be remiss if we didn't give a moment to the Mayan golden age of 250–900, when the Mayan civilization dominated the region and left behind massive stone cites such as Chichen Itza, which still survive.

THE OBSIDIAN MIRROR

We don't know much about the Mayans' rise to power, and we don't know much about why they began to abandon their cities. We do know that for about six and a half centuries, the Mayans were the largest, most powerful, and most thoroughly developed civilization in the Americas. Their art and architecture rivaled that of their

European, Asian, and African contemporaries, and their military and economic power was significant.

There were still some Mayan settlements when the Spanish invaded the Americas during the early sixteenth century, and there are still people of Mayan ethnicity to this day. But for the most part, daily life in the early Mayan communities remains a mystery to us.

The 2012 Prophecy

As midnight approached as December 21, 2012, began, many eyes were on the ancient Mayans. Conventional wisdom, boosted by New Age punditry (nearly 200 books were written about the prospect of a 2012 doomsday), held that the Mayans had expected the world to end on this very date. The truth is that most versions of the Mayan calendar didn't even end on December 21, 2012, and the ones that did made no explicit connection between the end of the calendar and the end of the world.

The well-preserved Mayan stone ruins of Chichen Itza, located in the dense jungles of Mexico's Yucatan peninsula, provide a rare glimpse of what it might have been like to live in a Mayan community a thousand years ago. The name *Chichen Itza* can be loosely translated as "at the mouth of the sacred waters": the waters in question were the two massive cenotes, or groundwater-filled sinkholes, located near the city. The most recognizable building in Chichen Itza proper is the ninety-eight-foot-tall Pyramid of Kukulcan, with gray stone staircases leading up to a square chapel at the top. Chichen Itza also features a low-tech observatory, numerous other distinctive temples (each with a different purpose), and the largest surviving ballcourt in the Mesoamerican world. Other Mayan cities lay unexplored, even undiscovered, but Chichen Itza alone has told us volumes about the world of the ancient Mayans and the rich ceremonial culture they created.

ISLAM AND THE NEW MIDDLE EAST

The Holy Prophet's Decree

"All those who listen to me shall pass on my words to others, and those to others again; and may the last ones understand my words better than those who listen to me directly."

—From the final sermon of the Prophet Muhammad (570–632)

If it were possible to survey the religious identities of most of the people of the world in the seventh century, regional pagan and folk religions would be in first place by a county mile. Over the next fourteen centuries, Christianity and Islam expanded to the point where, today, adherents of those two faiths make up more than half the world's population.

This shift in ideology wasn't accidental. It reflected the way that empires practicing Christianity in Western Europe, and Islam in the Middle East, carved up and colonized the world. Over subsequent centuries, these empires—and, by implication, their faiths—would become sworn enemies, an ironic fate for two religions founded by Jesus and Muhammad, figures who dedicated their lives to giving prophetic witness against the oppressions and violent hypocrisies of their time.

THE MECCAN WARS

There's a cautionary tale embedded in the stories of the big three Western monotheisms: be careful who you oppress. The Babylonians oppressed the Jewish people, and the Babylonians fell to the Persians. The same Roman Empire that crucified Jesus ultimately converted officially to the Christian faith. And the Quraysh tribe in Mecca and its allies needlessly harassed a small, harmless religious movement, only to witness that movement raise an army and conquer the entire Arabian Peninsula.

The conquests of the Prophet Muhammad (ca. 570–632) illustrate how a movement for self-defense can transform into an empire. There is no indication that he had any military aspirations; he just didn't want to follow the Meccan folk religion, which he and his followers regarded as idolatrous. At the age of forty, Muhammad reported that he had begun to hear the voice of the angel Gabriel, messenger of God, and he solemnly wrote down what he had been told, in the tradition of the Jewish prophets, in a series of texts we now call the Qur'an ("recitation"). Central to that message is the unity of God, a message Sunni Muslims would later recite in the *shahada* (profession of faith): *la ilaha illa'llah* ("there is no god but God"). And like the Jewish prophets before him, Muhammad was drawn by this message to walk a new road and preach a new, radically monotheistic faith that could not be reconciled with the traditions of the religious communities around him.

After being violently driven out of Mecca, the early Muslims secured a peace treaty—only to see that treaty dismissed two years later, after the Quraysh had incorrectly assumed that the Muslim movement had died down. Early Muslims soon discovered what many other small militant movements learn: once you've raised a good-sized army for self-defense, you'll end up having to keep it (because other regional powers will feel threatened by its size). By the time he passed away in 632, Muhammad left behind a generation of experienced soldiers who would rule the Rashidun and Umayyad Caliphates, empires that would—by 750—dominate the entire Middle East and Southern Mediterranean, from Afghanistan in the east to Spain and Morocco in the west. And for the fourteen centuries since, Islam has remained the dominant faith in the region.

Tawhid and Shirk

Two core values that were important even to early Islamic philosophy, due to the prominent role they play in the Qur'an, are *tawhid* (unity) and *shirk* (partnering). Both refer specifically to a person's attitude toward Allah, or God: tawhid recognizes the uniqueness of Allah, while shirk dilutes his power by suggesting that Allah has collaborators, or even superiors. Idolatry and polytheism are obviously a form of shirk, but human arrogance—particularly our tendency to display our own religiosity in a self-promotional way—can also qualify as shirk.

THE GLORY OF THE SASSANIDS

King of Kings

"Isfahan is half the world."

—Sassanid proverb

If you know your Roman history, you know the Parthian Empire—which ruled over what we now call Iran, Iraq, Syria, and much of the surrounding territory for a little over four centuries, from about 247 B.C.E. until around C.E. 224—was indirectly responsible for creating the Roman Empire by killing the beloved general Crassus. What you may not realize is that Rome never really avenged his death, and this is largely because Rome *couldn't*; the Parthians' well-trained (male and female) horse archers slaughtered legionaries at a safe distance and left survivors with a lifetime of nightmares. When the Parthian Empire fell apart and the Sassanids took over in 224, they inherited the Parthians' formidable military traditions and held their ground for another four centuries. They would also subject the Romans to a humiliation that even the Parthians never achieved: the actual capture and permanent imprisonment of a sitting Roman emperor.

When the Sassanid Empire did finally fall in 651, it marked the end of Zoroastrianism as a major world religious power, which was replaced by Islam. But for eight centuries (four under the Parthians and four under the Sassanids), Zoroastrianism rivaled Christianity and Roman paganism as an imperial ideology—and the legacy the Sassanids left behind in their age still quietly resonates in our own.

RESTORING ACHAEMENID GLORY

The Sassanids came to power in much the same way that small Persian states tended to do: from within. During a drawn-out dispute between Parthian rulers, the aptly titled Ardashir the Unifier (180–242) began gathering power in southern provinces, ultimately overthrowing the existing power structure. But it's his son, Shapur the Great (ca. 215–272), who brought the Roman Empire to its knees at the Battle of Edessa in 260.

As you may remember from an earlier chapter, the Roman Empire was in a volatile position during the middle of the third century. Emperor Valerian (ca. 193–260) successfully fought off opposition and established some credibility for himself, but as an older man living in Caesar's shadow he had to prove himself as a general on the battlefield. Unfortunately for him, the Sassanids had just as much to prove. They easily won the battle, capturing the emperor and his staff along with tens of thousands of soldiers. The Roman Empire had lost its emperor to an unassailable Persian Empire, with no hope of rescuing him.

Arda Viraf

The *Arda Viraf* ("Viraf the just"), which was probably written during the Sassanid period, tells the story of a devout Zoroastrian who travels to heaven and hell and returns to Earth to report what he found. Several centuries later, Dante Alighieri (1265–1341) would write a similar but much longer work, the *Divine Comedy*, from a Christian perspective.

What became of Valerian and his men afterward isn't entirely clear, though the majority of sources suggest that he was allowed to live out his remaining years relatively comfortably in exile. The empire that captured him would go on to outlast the Roman Empire itself by two centuries. The Sassanids, like the Parthians before them, would ultimately have the last laugh in their longstanding conflict with Rome.

THE UNITY OF JAPAN

The Rise of the Rising Sun

"When I look up into the vast sky tonight,
is it the same moon
that I saw rising
from behind Mt. Mikasa
at Kasuga Shrine
all those years ago?"
—Abe no Nakamaro (698–770), scholar and poet

We fundamentally misunderstand the history of ancient Japan if we think of it as a country, or even a continent. It would be more accurate to think of it as a planet. After all, the ancient Shinto holy text—the Kojiki—speaks of a supernatural origin for the eight islands that made up the Japanese milieu. The Japanese of antiquity were not mere tribes among others. They were the nations of their own world.

When the people of Japan did move westward to the Asian continent for diplomacy and trade, they called their homeland Nihon—literally "sun birth"—as a way of pointing out that Japan lies east, where the sun rises over the Pacific. The Japanese red circle flag, and the popular nickname "Land of the Rising Sun," are both just alternate ways of saying Nihon.

JAPAN ALONE, AND JAPAN AMONG NATIONS

The world of the Kojiki creation narrative is the world of Shinto, the most traditional Japanese religion and the only major world religion indigenous to the country. But by the late sixth century, Chinese culture—and, with it, Confucianism, Taoism, and Buddhism—had begun to migrate to the far-eastern islands of Asia, and had a profound effect on the society and government of Japan.

Far from rejecting the story of Shinto and the ancient Japanese identity, however, the culture of the period appeared to blend these traditions with relatively little conflict. While there was a gradual transition toward a Confucian approach to bureaucracy, and monarchs were increasingly drawn to Buddhist philosophy, Shinto remained—and, in some ways, still remains—the ceremonial civic religion of Japan. It is not unusual for a Buddhist in Japan today to also attend Shinto services, and it was not unusual to do so 1,400 years ago either. In religion and in secular life, Japan has a dual identity: it is its own universe, and it is a nation among nations. These aren't two concepts held in tension; rather, they're both elements present in historical Japanese identity.

The Kojiki and Nihon Shoki

The two core historical texts in Shinto, the Kojiki and the Nihon Shoki, were both written during the early eighth century. They tell the story of the primordial creation of Japan's eight islands and the early rulers who established the land's most fundamental traditions.

This became especially evident during the Nara and Heian ("peace") periods (710–794 and 794–1185, respectively), as Japanese monarchs built new capitals in Nara and Kyoto that reflected both the ancestral traditions of the Japanese islands and the cultural and technological influences of the nation's Chinese trading partners. Royal succession during these periods was not especially cutthroat by historical standards, but the gradually increasing power of the aristocracy and the military classes did presage the power struggles that were to come.

THE VIKING CONQUESTS OF EUROPE

Norse by Norsewest

"Brothers shall fight and fell each other,
And sisters' sons shall kinship stain;
Hard is it on earth, with mighty whoredom;
Axe-time, sword-time, shields are sundered,
Wind-time, wolf-time, ere the world falls;
Nor ever shall men each other spare."

—From *Voluspo* (the Wise Woman's Prophecy)

The Vikings who raided Britain for several centuries during the Middle Ages were fast, terrifying, technologically sophisticated shipbuilders, and generally very difficult to defeat in combat. The question of why they went to the trouble of raiding Britain is one we've almost always answered badly. When almost any society on Earth does something violent, there's usually a very practical and somewhat undignified reason for it. Maybe they are desperate or resentful or frustrated or perhaps they are motivated by necessity. But when it comes to the Vikings, we look to the old *Eddas*, the sagas of Norse mythology, and declare that the Vikings were an honor-bound military culture that just loved to fight—Earth's answer to the Klingons from Star Trek. Most feared of all were the *berserkers* (Old Norse: "bearskin-shirted"), who were said to have drawn on the violent primal energy of the bears they ate, skinned, and revered.

But history suggests more down-to-earth explanations for the Viking conquests. Invaders from continental Europe had destabilized the regional Scandinavian economy and political structure. Political and economic changes in Denmark left untold thousands of soldiers displaced and hungry, and the soft, fleshy coasts of Europe were their feeding grounds.

BUTCHERS AND KINGS

The first sign of Viking trouble came in June 793, when a small group of Vikings made landfall on the tiny island of Lindisfarne in northern England, home of a monastery and little else. They slaughtered some monks, captured others, and left with all the loot they could carry. "The heathens poured out the blood of saints around the altar," one contemporary wrote, "and trampled on the bodies of saints in the temple of God, like dung in the street." The incident put Western Europe on notice, and kicked off three centuries of Viking conquests.

Saga

The word *saga*, referring to a complex epic, comes from the Old English root word *sagu*, meaning "saying." So while we think of the Norse sagas as self-described epics, the Norse used the word to refer to any story, epic or otherwise, that was made up of words.

The story of the Viking invasion of Britain definitively ended when the Viking king Harald Hardrada (1015–1066) took an arrow to the head at the Battle of Stamford Bridge in September 1066. Ironically, the victor in that battle, Harold Godwinson (1022–1066), was himself killed shortly afterward at the Battle of Hastings by the Normans, themselves descendants of Vikings. Evidence of Viking expansion stretches as far west as North America, where they established a colony centuries before Columbus "discovered" the continent, and as far east as Constantinople. The Vikings may be a millennium removed from their bloody conquests, but they will never be forgotten.

THE HOLY ROMAN EMPEROR

Charlemagne and the New European Monarchy

"You nobles, you sons of my leading men, soft and dandified, trusting in your birth and your wealth, paying no attention to my command and your advancement, you neglected the pursuit of learning and indulged yourselves in the sport of pleasure and idleness and foolish pastimes. By the King of the heavens I think nothing of your nobility and your beauty. Others can admire you. Know this without any doubt: unless you rapidly make up for your idleness by eager effort, you will never receive any benefit from Charlemagne."

—Charlemagne (ca. 747–814), as quoted (probably inaccurately) in Notker the Stammerer's unreliable but deeply entertaining biography, *De Carolo Magno* (ca. 883)

Ah, chivalry! If you grew up reading medieval fantasy novels, playing *Dungeons & Dragons,* or listening to cheesy 1970s progressive rock ballads, then there's probably a part of you that still imagines Europe of a millennium ago as a very interesting place. Armored knights on horseback with lances, fair damsels in steepled headdresses, and talk of dragons!

Not many people in the Middle Ages had the luxury of being chivalrous, at least not in the glamorous way we remember. But there is a basis in history for the idea we now think of as chivalry. Central to it was a man forever known to history as Charlemagne.

THE PAPAL NATIONS

You can call him Charles (686–741) if you like, because Charlemagne just means "Charles the Great." After inheriting the Frankish kingdom from his father, the less impressively titled Pepin the Short (714–768), Charles began decades of warfare across both Christian central Europe and Muslim Spain. In 800, he had so completely established his military and political reputation that Pope Leo III, at a ceremony at St. Peter's Basilica in Rome, declared Charles to be a new Caesar Augustus and emperor of the Holy Roman Empire in the West.

This cemented Charlemagne's legacy, but it had an even greater effect on the papacy. There was, of course, no longer a literal Roman Empire for Charlemagne and his successors to rule, but by declaring the Christian church to be the rightful successor of Rome itself, Pope Leo III transformed Christianity from a faith of the crucified into a faith that had the power *to* crucify. He also dramatically strengthened his own position. For the next millennium, the papacy would remain a major power broker in European politics—with the pope himself being someone who could legitimize or destroy monarchs at will.

Despite his brutal treatment of Muslims, pagans, and heretics, Charlemagne was a gentleman to most other Christians in good standing and even, some accounts suggest, to Jews. Stories of his courage and generosity live on in the literature of the Middle Ages, where he is presented as a model—and, in many respects, *the* model—of medieval Christian leadership. Several centuries later, the example he set would even be used to justify the Crusades.

But this reputation is a little misleading. Charlemagne only reigned as Holy Roman Emperor for thirteen years; he had proved to be far more effective as a conqueror than an administrator, and when he passed in 814, the personality cult he left behind placed his son, Louis the Pious (778–840), in an unmanageable position. Despite fending off multiple rebellions and three full-fledged civil wars, Louis technically died with his empire intact—but it broke apart less than five years later as his sons, Charlemagne's grandsons, fought over control. Pope Leo III's promise of a Christian Augustus to unite the West, and a reconstructed Holy Roman Empire to rule over it, had not taken into account the empire-shattering power of sibling rivalry.

The Nine Worthies

Centuries after Charlemagne's reign, troubadours celebrated a code of chivalry that focused on following the good examples set by nine brave men who were often described as the Nine Worthies: three pagans (Hector from *The Iliad*, Julius Caesar, and Alexander the Great), three Jews (Joshua, David, and the third-century B.C.E. Jewish revolutionary Judas Maccabeus), and three Christians (Charlemagne, the possibly fictional King Arthur, and the French crusader Godfrey of Bouillon). As the only known historical Christian monarch among the Worthies, Charlemagne remained a symbol of Christian Europe for centuries to come.

THE GREAT SCHISM OF 1054

East Is East and West Is West

"Let them be anathema Maranatha with the Simoniacs, Valesians, Arians, Donatists, Nicolaitists, Severians, Pneumatomachoi, Manichaeans, Nazarenes, and all the heretics—nay, with the devil himself and his angels, unless they should repent. AMEN, AMEN, AMEN."
—Abbot Humbert of Silva Candida (d. 1061), legate to Pope Leo IX, in his 1054 letter excommunicating the Patriarch of Constantinople and his flock

---

At the time it happened, the East-West Schism of 1054 (the break of communion between the Western Roman Catholic and Eastern Orthodox churches) didn't seem like a really big deal. Rome and Constantinople were 850 miles apart to begin with, so geography alone had already divided the church to some extent, and there was no reason to believe that the schism would be as universal or as permanent as it has turned out to be. But it was this event—marked not by a series of battles or natural disasters, but by a series of letters and theological disagreements—that ultimately closed the book on the Roman Empire's influence (more precisely, the *Eastern* Roman Empire's influence) in Western Europe.

So complete was the existing rift between the East and the West that the Schism was a relatively minor event at the time it happened. It was only in later centuries, as the Crusades and conflict between Christian and Islamic Europe triangulated the East into a series of uncomfortable diplomatic and military positions, that the full weight of the Schism was felt. Now, almost a thousand years later, the separation between the Western Roman Catholic and Eastern Orthodox churches feels permanent—the traditions having become so different from each other, in liturgy and theology, that they would both be completely transformed by any sort of equitable merger.

Five Nontheological Reasons for the East-West Schism

1. **Obedience.** As noted in the previous chapter, the papacy was acquiring a great deal of political power in Western Europe during the Middle Ages, but by 1054 Constantinople had a political power structure of its own, and this gave it more independence than the Western church was comfortable with.

2. **Politics.** As demonstrated one hundred fifty years later with the sacking of Constantinople, the political interests of Western Europe and those of Eastern Europe were not necessarily well-aligned anyway. A succession of popes had made it their mission for centuries to unite the Christian West into the Church's own Holy Roman Empire, bucking diplomatic protocol by calling Charlemagne *their* emperor rather than honoring the legitimacy of the Eastern Roman Empire.

3. **Location, location, location.** As noted earlier, Rome and Constantinople were 850 miles apart. Delivering messages between the two took a great deal of time, which factored into the obedience and political entanglement issues—how can the Eastern church know what to do, or who to support, when it's so far away from the seat of power?

4. **Western Roman influence.** The Eastern church was fundamentally Greek in character, while the Western church

wrapped itself very consciously in the iconography and history of the old Roman Empire.

5. **Constantine himself.** As noted in a previous chapter, the emperor Constantine the Great (272–337) established Constantinople to be a second secular *and* religious capital of the Roman Empire. By keeping the seat of Christian power in Rome, the Western church appeared to defy the wishes of the first Christian emperor.

Heresy and Excommunication

Although the word *heresy* is often used to describe any difference of opinion with the ruling theological authority, the term is usually reserved for people whose disagreements with the church are so severe as to interfere with their ability to participate in the Sacraments. In early Christian history, those deemed heretics were excommunicated (forbidden from receiving Communion or claiming membership in the church) until they repented. Those who have been excommunicated are declared *anathema* ("sacrificed")—left to God to do with as he wishes, without the church's intercession.

THE CRUSADES AND THE SPANISH INQUISITION

The Violent Radicalism of Medieval Christianity

"Kill them all, for the Lord knoweth them that are his."
—Credibly attributed to Arnaud Amalric (d. 1225), papal legate to Pope Innocent III, after he was asked by soldiers how to treat civilians in Beziers, a religiously diverse city that included both orthodox and heretical Christians. In a subsequent letter, Amalric himself boasted that 20,000 men, women, and children ("irrespective of rank, sex, or age") were slaughtered on his orders, and the city was burned to the ground.

In contemporary times we've gotten used to the concept of the "problem religion"—a religion whose adherents don't get along with the contemporary world and are driven to respond to it in violent ways. Every major religion has filled this role in some place, at some time, but there is something especially ironic about the fact that institutions representing a religion founded in the name of Jesus Christ, who opposed both the accumulation of wealth and all forms of violence, were led for centuries by grotesquely wealthy powerbrokers whose ambitions revolved around large-scale violence.

CRUSADES OF BLOOD

There is a tendency in Western history to portray Christianity as good and Islam as evil, and every historian has to reckon with that tendency. There is no question that both religions have had their share of violent fanatics. There is also no question that, in the Middle Ages, Christianity was by far the more violent and less tolerant of the two.

But is it really fair to blame Christianity, or credit Islam, for a pattern of history that predates both religions? The Romans were, after all, hostile toward local faiths that posed a challenge to supremacy of the imperial civic religion, and the Christian empires were—quite consciously and explicitly—inheritors of the Roman tradition. Meanwhile, the Islamic nations of the Middle Ages inherited the culture of the Persian empires—most of which were noted for their religious tolerance, their opposition to slavery, their relatively progressive views on gender, and so on. Taking these histories into account, the Crusades seem almost inevitable.

Crusade and Jihad

Two words that are treated as synonyms in global politics, and decidedly aren't, are *crusade* and *jihad*. The term *crusade* was coined in the late Middle Ages to refer colloquially to the cross (French: *croisée*) worn by crusaders—a reference to their fashion, not their ideology. *Jihad*, which is simply the Arabic word for "struggle," is often used to refer to war (even a defensive war fought for secular reasons), but it can also be used in a general sense to refer to almost anything else that involves effort.

Pope Urban II (1042–1099) called for the First Crusade in 1095, asking Western Christians to reunite with their Eastern brothers and sisters to repel Turkish Muslim invaders. If this had actually happened, the history of the region would have been very different—but the Christian army, once assembled, soon turned its attention to the more interesting proposition of conquering Jerusalem. By the time the Fourth Crusade rolled around in 1202, Western Christians themselves invaded Constantinople for money—conquering it, looting it, and generally treating it much worse than actual Muslim invaders probably would have. When what was left of Byzantium fell to the Ottoman Empire in 1453, Western institutional Christianity couldn't be bothered to interfere; it was too busy with, well, the Spanish Inquisition.

AN INQUISITION OF TERROR

With apologies to the comedy group Monty Python, a lot of people expected the Spanish Inquisition. When Queen Isabella and King Ferdinand II issued the Alhambra Decree in 1492 requiring Jewish and Muslim residents of one of the most religiously diverse nations on Earth to convert to Christianity or leave, it stood to reason that people who converted might not feel a sincere personal conversion experience. Muslim and Jewish converts, called Marranos, were especially subject to scrutiny.

Tomás de Torquemada (1420–1498), appointed the Roman Catholic Church's Grand Inquisitor for Spain in 1483, was happy to give them that scrutiny. Over the next several centuries the Inquisition would harass, surveil, publicly humiliate, and sometimes execute those whom its leaders believed did not practice the Christian faith, or did not practice it correctly.

A typical record entry from August 1635 notes the detention of one Joan Compte, age fifty-five, who was interrogated until he revealed that he had once witnessed a man eating bacon and onions on the day before the feast of St. Bartholomew, a day that the church had set aside for fasting. At that point he was free to go. This was the Inquisition's approach from the beginning: detain random individuals, make them believe that their own lives were in danger, and then release them only if they betray their neighbors. This served both a religious and secular purpose: it made Spain a hostile place for religious minorities, which pleased the Roman Catholic Church, and it made Spanish citizens feel as if they were constantly being watched and could trust no one, which pleased the monarchy. While the primary targets of the Inquisition's behavior were initially Jews and Muslims, it quickly became clear that anyone who criticized the political or religious authority in the days of the Inquisition was taking his life in his hands.

The Treaty of Granada

In late November 1491 the Spanish government persuaded the independent Islamic state of Granada to sign a peace treaty that granted the Catholic monarchs control over Spain. In exchange Spain agreed to allow Muslims in the region to practice their religion freely. They violated the treaty just four months later, banning Jews and Muslims from Spain with the Alhambra Decree.

THE CALIPHATE OF CÓRDOBA

How al-Andalus Saved Western Civilization

"I have now reigned above fifty years in victory or peace; beloved by my subjects, dreaded by my enemies, and respected by my allies. Riches and honors, power and pleasure, have waited on my call, nor does any earthly blessing appear to have been wanting to my felicity; in this situation I have diligently numbered the days of pure and genuine happiness which have fallen to my lot; they amount to fourteen. O man! Place not thy confidence in this present world."

—Abd-ar-Rahman III (891–961), emir and caliph of Córdoba

What Greece was to the classical world, al-Andalus was to the Middle Ages. From about 720 until the late fifteenth century—an immense scale of time—the southern two-thirds of the Spanish peninsula operated under the rule of a relatively tolerant, scholarly tradition of Islamic theocracy. The people of al-Andalus functionally invented astronomy and mathematics as we have come to know them, and both Jewish and Islamic theology flourished there, as did trade.

FROM THE UMAYYAD CALIPHATE TO THE FITNA

It's easy to forget that the Prophet Muhammad had been dead for less than a century when the Umayyad Caliphate, one of the two empires that emerged in the wake of his death, conquered Spain in 711. The Umayyad Caliphate brought with it respect for literacy, a history of experiencing religious persecution, and cultural influence from a region that had been at times Persian or Carthaginian, but never as entirely Roman as the nations of central Europe.

Al-Andalus would ultimately fragment into thirty-three different kingdoms during the period of *fitna* (Arabic: "affliction"), after the fall of the caliphate in 1031. But these kingdoms would themselves prove surprisingly durable. Al-Andalus did not return to Christian control until the late fifteenth century, at which point Queen Isabella and King Ferdinand II—dedicated opponents of Islam—took it upon themselves to purge seven centuries of history from the Iberian Peninsula. And despite the shockingly violent tactics they used, they never quite succeeded. The legacy of Muslim Spain remains an inviolable part of the peninsula's history.

THE MYSTERY OF GREAT ZIMBABWE

A City of Gold and Stone

"I always tell people that if they want to know about the history of a country, do not go to the history books. Go to the fiction."

—Chenjerai Hove (1956–2015), poet

When the British-controlled nation in southern Africa then known as Rhodesia won its independence in 1980, leaders looked to the city's most famous artifact for its new name: Zimbabwe. Great Zimbabwe (Shona: "houses of stone") was a massive set of ruins well known to local nations but mysterious to Europe. First visiting the site in 1871, Western archaeologists initially believed that it had to have been built by foreigners—*had* to have been—but they eventually conceded in 1929, after extensive research and dozens of failed hypotheses, that it was in fact a product of the local communities. Reclaiming that legacy, and rescuing it from the misconceptions of imperial Europe, was an important symbolic step for the leaders of the young nation.

During its prime, from about 1100 until about 1450, Great Zimbabwe was a major city with eighteen thousand inhabitants. Its two main industries were gold and gold trading, and its more than four thousand gold mines produced an estimated 1.2 million pounds of gold—about 40 percent of the world's entire mined gold supply for several centuries. Its ruins are as impressive as those of any abandoned city. Outside of that, we know shockingly little about it. Given the sheer amount of gold it produced, and the demand that gold would have produced on the global market, this silence seems strange.

TIME'S ERASER

Over the course of this book you may have already gotten the sense that where a city is located largely determines how much we know about it. If it operated autonomously and with minimal interaction with global colonial powers, as the Olmecs did, then there was little need to record written histories of the region because oral historians were already there. When a civilization that has survived for centuries on oral tradition abruptly writes down its traditions, as the Israelites did during their period of Babylonian captivity, it's usually an ominous sign—an indication that the community fears cultural genocide and doesn't know if its stories will ever be told again. Written literature provides a time capsule for those stories.

But Great Zimbabwe, abandoned long before colonial empires scrambled for African territory, didn't need that kind of time capsule; its stories likely live on among the Shona peoples, although there are numerous other local candidates who could have preserved them as well. There's the problem, when you get right down to it: Zimbabwe is so diverse that we can't really know exactly who to identify as the heirs to Great Zimbabwe. They're probably the Shona, but we can't be sure. One reason is that Zimbabwe has sixteen official languages. And it's possible that the true heirs of Great Zimbabwe actually migrated to a neighboring territory that we might now call South

Africa or Zambia. Communities of the fifteenth century would have had no way, and in any case no incentive, to respect political boundaries of the twenty-first.

We can take further steps to determine exactly who the original inhabitants of Great Zimbabwe were and how they lived—remains that can be DNA-tested, writings from neighboring countries that have yet to be discovered and/or translated, oral traditions that have not yet been recorded—but it's possible that, even when we've exhausted all of the evidence left behind by this civilization, we won't be any closer to learning the untold stories of this once-powerful city.

GENGHIS KHAN AND THE TRIUMPH OF THE MONGOLS

The Earth's Greatest Conqueror

"If the cairn were not built, the magpie wouldn't have perched."

—Mongolian proverb

Until the twentieth century, historians measured man-made atrocities by the bloody yardstick of Genghis Khan (1162–1227). Depending on whose account you read, Khan's conquests—which led to the largest land empire in human history, dwarfing those of the Spanish, the Romans, Napoleon, and Alexander the Great—took the lives of anywhere between ten and forty million people.

Against that backdrop, it seems strange to talk about what Genghis Khan accomplished. But we do it all the time when we're talking about Europeans who settled the Americas, wiping out indigenous communities wholesale while they were at it. History for the most part is the study of strange things. And there's nothing stranger than the empire Genghis Khan left behind—an uninterrupted mass of land stretching from the Caspian Sea in the west to the Pacific Ocean in the east. Before Genghis Khan, conquest on this scale was impossible. *After* Genghis Khan, conquest on this scale was impossible. It is likely that for the remainder of human history, he—and only he—will know what it is like to succeed so thoroughly in conquest.

Conquering vast amounts of territory is one thing; holding on to them forever is another. By the end of the fourteenth century, the Mongol Empire as such had broken down into a cluster of smaller empires, and then it disintegrated completely. But the effects of the Mongol conquests were far from ephemeral; when Genghis Khan's armies swept across central Asia, they created trade routes that still exist, in some form, to this day. The Northern Yuan dynasty, located in what we now call Mongolia, remained a significant regional power until 1635.

The Great Khan's Daughters

Genghis Khan's army included both women and men, unusual by the standards of the time, and he gave special care in training his daughters for military leadership. One of his oldest daughters, Alakhai Bekhi, ruled over his Chinese territories while he conquered elsewhere; another, Alaltun Bekhi, administered Uyghur territories he conquered in modern-day Turkey.

THE GRISLY HARVEST OF THE BLACK DEATH

Europe's Doomsday

"In what annals has it ever been read that houses were left vacant, cities deserted, the country neglected, the fields too small for the dead and a fearful and universal solitude over the whole earth?...Oh happy people of the future, who have not known these miseries..."

—Francesco "Petrarch" Petrarca (1304–1374), poet

Between 1347 and 1353 as many as one hundred million people died horribly from an epidemic of the plague, which we now know was caused by a specific bacterium identified as *Yersinia pestis* (*Y. pestis*). Victims would experience fever, grotesquely swollen lymph nodes, convulsions, and—within a matter of days—death. Not everyone who contracted the disease died, but most did, and it was an especially painful and undignified way to die. The Flemish scientist Simon de Covinus, writing at the height of the epidemic, gave us the name we now remember it by: *mors atra*, the Black Death.

The effect of the Black Death on Europe, where one-third to one-half of the total population died from the disease in about five years, was especially profound. But the epidemic tore through cities on three continents, leaving in its wake a deeply rooted cultural fear of disease that still affects us to this day.

THE PRIMORDIAL KILLER

The plague may be as old as humanity itself. Before our ancestors could read and write, before the first empires spread, its shadow hung over us.

In October 2015, biologists sequenced raw DNA in a 5,000-year-old Russian human tooth and found evidence of ancient *Y. pestis* bacteria, an infection that had almost certainly caused the death of its host.

Scientists have long speculated that the plague may have played a role in prehistoric human migration and in ancient history. In the Hebrew Bible, 1 Samuel 5:6 speaks of a deadly plague marked by "sores" and (in the Septuagint, an ancient Greek translation of the Hebrew Bible) by the appearance of mice, a telltale characteristic for a disease that is often spread by fleas. Thucydides's description of the Plague of Athens in the fifth century B.C.E., a disease he claims to have himself survived, bears symptoms consistent with those of both typhoid fever and plague and has been attributed at various times to both.

But the first large-scale plague epidemic we can be certain about arrived in 541 in Constantinople and surrounding cities along the Mediterranean. In what later became known as the Justinian Plague, the disease killed tens of millions of people in a matter of years. There had never been a documented outbreak of comparable size before, and for those who lived through it the scale of the epidemic must have seemed like the stuff of apocalyptic prophecy. Unfortunately, the end of the world would come again.

FROM HOPEI TO CONSTANTINOPLE

The earliest record of the epidemic we now remember as the Black Death comes from the Hopei province of northwestern China, where a mysterious disease killed the majority of the local population in 1331. Similar reports peppered China, India, and Mongol military records through the 1330s and 1340s, but it was not until Mongol forces engaged an Italian army fortifying the port city of Caffa, now known as the Ukrainian city of Feodosia, that the crowded network of European naval trading routes carried the plague through the European continent.

Disease in a Germless World

Taking their cue from the Roman physician Galen of Pergamon (130–210), most medieval Europeans believed diseases were spread by scent and that other strong smells, like flowers or rotting fruit, could block the odor of disease and prevent contamination. Germs were not identified until the nineteenth century.

Historians disagree on whether the Mongol army intended to spread the plague. The Italian lawyer Gabriele de Mussis (ca. 1280–1356) suggested that the Mongol general Janibeg Khan, noticing his men were falling prey to the disease, catapulted their corpses into the city "in hopes that the intolerable stench would kill everyone inside"; since it's unlikely that an invading military commander would share his hopes with an enemy civilian, this seems speculative at best. In any case, whether the spread of the plague was accidental or was an intentional act of biological warfare, the damage was done. Genoese traders soon set sail for Constantinople, exposing every major port city in Europe, and some beyond it, to one of history's deadliest diseases.

THE PLAGUE PITS OF EUROPE

For a variety of reasons Europe of 1347 was especially vulnerable to the plague. A sophisticated trading network guaranteed the spread of any contagious disease that reached a port city. In turn, these cities—filthy, densely packed, and swarming with rats—provided an ideal incubator for germs, and a hub by which nearby rural communities could also be exposed to the disease. And Europe was only a generation removed from the Great Famine of 1315, which had already killed some 15 percent of the population over a seven-year period and left survivors understandably anxious to protect their economic and agricultural assets, even at the risk of disease.

During 1348 and 1349 every major city in Western Europe became a plague town. The bodies of the dead became too numerous to bury, often necessitating mass graves called plague pits. Poland, Belgium, and the Netherlands were largely spared at first, probably because they didn't participate as actively in regional trade routes, but mini-epidemics over the next several centuries, such as the Italian Plague of 1629 and London's Great Plague of 1665, would gradually expose the entire European continent to the disease.

PRAYERS FOR THE DEAD

The scale of the Black Death outside of Europe is hard to assess, but we know for certain that it killed tens of millions of people throughout Asia and the Middle East during the mid-fourteenth century. China and India suffered even before the disease reached Europe's coastal cities, and its presence in Constantinople made disease a consequence of trade. The Black Death had reached Egypt by the end of 1347, Jerusalem by 1348, Mecca by 1349. No region or demographic was spared.

The plague has never disappeared; it continues to affect us to this day, with several hundred cases reported to the World Health Organization each year. The disease is treatable with antibiotics but still carries a high mortality rate in rural areas of the developing world, where medical technology and sanitation infrastructure are not always sufficient to keep it at bay. International nonprofits have taken aggressive measures over the past several years to contain the spread of the disease in rural Madagascar, especially, where the plague remains a mysterious and terrifying killer.

THE HOLY SLEEP OF BYZANTIUM

The Last of the Roman Emperors

"[I]t occurs to me that what I am now about to tell will seem neither probable nor plausible to future generations, especially as time flows on and my story becomes ancient history. I fear they may think me a writer of fiction, and even put me among the poets."

—Procopius of Caesarea (ca. 500–554), from his *Secret History*

Rome died twice. In the West paganism gave way to Christianity and the centralized Roman Empire broke into smaller regional states. In the East, Christianity gave way to Islam and the dominant cultural influences there shifted from those of Western Europe to those of the Middle East. The year 1453, when Constantinople fell to the Ottoman Empire, marked the end of the Roman Empire.

Although numerous future nations would describe themselves as heir to the Romans, this claim invariably comes off as either ominous or pathetic. Roman dominance over the West, like a lot of things in history, was unique; once its time has passed, it can't be recaptured. You just had to be there. And after 1453, nobody was.

WHO GAVE CONSTANTINOPLE THE WORKS?

Although the event that arguably put an end to Constantinople as a global power was its defeat at the hands of Western Christians in the Fourth Crusade of 1204, several factors contributed to the city's collapse. The Great Schism of 1054 effectively isolated it from the nations (and massive armies) of Christian Western Europe, leaving it more or less unprotected in its wars with the emerging Islamic nations of the Middle East. Most of the factors that contributed to the collapse of Western Rome, which I've described previously, also apply to its Eastern counterpart. In the end, the Byzantine Empire was too big to protect and too ambitious to sustain.

Empress Theodora

The Empress Theodora (ca. 500–548), wife and co-regent of Emperor Justinian I, was a powerful and influential leader in her own right. She demonstrated her influence during the Nika Riots in 532; when Justinian and his advisors contemplated fleeing the palace in the face of public revolt, Theodora demanded that they remain in the palace despite the risk to their personal safety. The rest deferred. After Justinian's army successfully suppressed the revolt, her decision had been vindicated. The crowd had already selected a new emperor to replace Justinian and likely would have crowned him if Justinian had fled.

The Great Sphinx of Giza, sculpted during Egypt's Old Kingdom in the third millennium B.C.E., depicts a figure with the head of a human and the body of a lion. It was probably built by the pharaoh Khafre, who is also credited with building the Pyramid of Khafre (often called the Second Pyramid). Although it used to be said that Napoleon's soldiers shot off the Sphinx's nose for target practice, this is incorrect. The nose was missing well before the French emperor arrived in Egypt in 1798.

Photo Credit: © Getty Images/holgs

Among the earliest civilizations were those of Mesopotamia, which formed around the fourth century B.C.E. Between 911 and 612 B.C.E., the dominant power in the region was the Assyrian empire, which eventually extended its rule across much of the eastern Mediterranean and the Middle East. The Assyrians worshipped a pantheon of gods, one of whom appears in this bas-relief.

Photo Credit: © Getty Images/Gilmanshin

High above Athens, on the north side of its acropolis, stands the Erechtheion, a temple dedicated to the deities Poseidon and Athena. It was built in the fifth century B.C.E., and is an outstanding example of classical Greek art, particularly the Porch of the Maidens (shown here), which uses the statues of six women as supporting pillars.

In Mesoamerica (an area extending from central Mexico to Belize) there are a series of giant sculpted heads. These are remnants of the Olmec civilization, which flourished sometime before the tenth century B.C.E. They were the first major cultural force in this area. The heads probably show important individuals in the Olmec world.

The Great Wall of China was intended to protect the Middle Kingdom from raids by northern barbarians. It was constructed over many centuries, beginning in the seventh century B.C.E. Originally there were many different walls, which were gradually joined together to make a single fortification, extending more than 3,800 miles.

Photo Credit: © Getty Images/Nikada

In many parts of northern India the edicts of King Ashoka are written on pillars. He ruled the area in the third century B.C.E. as a member of the Maurya Empire, which presided over the Indian subcontinent between 322 B.C.E. and 187 B.C.E. His edicts, of which only thirty-three survive, discuss religious matters and give us some of the first tangible evidence of Buddhism, one of the world's great religious traditions.

Photo Credit: © Getty Images/Rufous52

On March 15, 44 B.C.E., in one of the most famous murders in history, Julius Caesar was killed by a group of his fellow Roman senators. His assassins feared he was about to become emperor for life and destroy the Republic. They weren't far off; Caesar had already functionally destroyed the checks and balances of the old Roman Republic, and his nephew Octavian (63 B.C.E.–C.E. 14), better known as Augustus, became the first emperor of the new Roman Empire.

Photo Credit: © Getty Images/aaronizer

The Church of the Holy Sepulchre in Jerusalem's old quarter encloses two of Christianity's holiest spots: the site of Jesus' crucifixion and the place of his tomb, from which, Scripture says, he was resurrected. The central part of the church itself dates to the fourth century and is shared between a number of denominations, including Greek Orthodox, Armenian Orthodox, Roman Catholic, and Coptic, which is an Egyptian branch of Christianity.

Photo Credit: © Getty Images/efesenko

The Mayan people originated in Mesoamerica around 2000 B.C.E. and developed a sophisticated civilization that included a complex writing system, calendar, extensive art work (such as the mask shown here), mathematics, and astronomical observatories. Ruins of Mayan cities have been found throughout the region.

Photo Credit: © Getty Images/ManuelVelasco

The Kaaba at Mecca is the holiest shrine in Islam. Each year hundreds of thousands of Muslims travel to the holy city. This pilgrimage (hajj) is one of the five pillars of Islam. Once there, pilgrims walk seven times around the Kaaba in a counterclockwise direction. The eastern cornerstone of the Kaaba is the Black Stone, which, according to Muslim legend, goes back to the time of Adam and Eve and was placed in the wall by the Prophet Muhammad (ca. 570–632).

Photo Credit: © Getty Images/ramzihachicho

For three hundred years, beginning in the 790s, the people known as the Vikings swept over Western Europe. They traveled as far afield as Constantinople to the east and to the shores of North America to the west. One group, known as the Rus, gave their name to Russia. Another settled on a peninsula in France, which eventually became Normandy (land of the Northmen). Still others conquered large parts of Britain, creating the Danelaw, a region ruled by Scandinavian kings.

In the year 800, Pope Leo III (750–816) crowned Charlemagne, king of the Franks (shown here), Roman Emperor, making him the greatest power in Western Europe. His empire did not last long after his death and was divided among his sons into what eventually became France, Germany, and Alsace-Lorraine, a strip of territory running north to south between the two.

The guillotine, invented in the eighteenth century as a humane means of execution, came into its own during the French Revolution. As the revolution went on, it launched a Reign of Terror against its enemies, and thousands died by the guillotine. In 1794, the leaders of the Terror were themselves arrested and beheaded.

The Second World War (1939–1945) ended in the explosions of atomic bombs over the Japanese cities of Hiroshima and Nagasaki. For the next forty-five years, East and West would be locked in a Cold War, threatening one another with nuclear weapons that could wipe out mankind.

From 1961 until 1989, the German city of Berlin was divided by a concrete wall that separated the eastern (Soviet dominated) section from the western (American dominated) sides. The wall was heavily guarded, and many East Berliners lost their lives trying to cross the wall into the West.

Photo Credit: © Getty Images/7000

The September 11, 2001, terrorist attacks by al-Qaeda on the United States were of the largest scale in human history. Since that time, the United States and its allies have grappled with different responses to international terrorism with varying degrees of success.

Photo Credit: © Getty Images/ramzihachicho

On July 20, 1969, astronaut Neil Armstrong became the first human to set foot on the surface of the moon. Armstrong's words upon stepping down from the *Apollo* 11 space capsule were, "That's one small step for [a] man, one giant leap for mankind."

Photo Credit: © Wikimedia Commons/NASA

THE GOLDEN AGE OF THE AZTECS

Heart of the Jaguar

"All the earth is a grave, and nought escapes it;
nothing is so perfect that it does not fall and disappear."

—Nezahualcoyotl (1402–1472), king of Texcoco

The Aztec Empire had existed for less than a century when Spanish explorers first discovered the Americas, and in that respect it was a very young empire. But as we have seen in the case of the Olmecs and the Mayans, it was a very young empire with a very old history. And the European conquistadors, missionaries, and financiers who arrived in the New World weren't just taking aim at the Aztecs; they were taking aim at that history too.

But for a time the Aztec Empire achieved a level of regional control that was remarkable by any standard. The political machinations they used to keep a loose coalition of city-states together were brilliant, and they were often as innovative in their shocking brutality as they were in their craftiness.

THE JAGUAR'S HEART

One of the first things you probably remember hearing about the Aztecs is that they practiced human sacrifice. This sounds like the sort of Spanish missionary propaganda that an empire would spread about the innocent community it's about to violently conquer, enslave, and exterminate, but in the case of the Aztecs it happens to be true. They did practice human sacrifice in the capital of Tenochtitlan. It served a practical purpose that, in the long run, could have actually saved lives. (Though that doesn't mean that human sacrifice is a good thing, and if I have to tell you that you should probably stop reading now and give this book to someone less impressionable.)

The Aztecs, like the Sumerians and early Greeks before them, ruled by hegemony: one city-state rules over other city-states as first among equals, despite them having independent governments. According to some historians, Aztec human sacrifice worked kind of like it did in the Hunger Games book and movie series: each city-state was responsible for bringing forward someone for sacrifice in the ruling city-state of Tenochtitlan, and the city-states would often compete, either to have the privilege (thereby doing away with a troublemaker and scoring points with the rulers and the gods) or to not have the privilege (because they didn't want to kill their own people). In either case, it gave city-states something to fight about among themselves without having bloody civil wars to reshape the hegemony every so often, like the aforementioned Sumerians and Greeks did.

Umbilical Cord Ritual

According to some texts, Aztecs believed that an infant's umbilical cord, which is rich in *tonalli* (cosmic energy, essentially), played a crucial role in reinforcing their gender role. The umbilical cord of a girl would be buried underneath the house, giving her homemakers' aptitude, while the umbilical cord of a boy would be buried on the battlefield, giving him the strength to defend himself.

EUROPE AND THE COLONIAL PROJECT

The Razor-Sharp Edge of the World

"Presently we discovered two or three villages, and the people all came down to the shore, calling out to us, and giving thanks to God. Some brought us water, and others victuals: others seeing that I was not disposed to land, plunged into the sea and swam out to us, and we perceived that they interrogated us if we had come from heaven. An old man came on board my boat; the others, both men and women cried with loud voices—'Come and see the men who have come from heavens. Bring them victuals and drink.' There came many of both sexes, every one bringing something, giving thanks to God, prostrating themselves on the earth, and lifting up their hands to heaven...I could conquer the whole of them with fifty men, and govern them as I pleased."
—Christopher Columbus, from his journal entry of October 14, 1492

Western Europe of the late fifteenth century was drunk on horror. Little more than a hundred years removed from its near extermination at the hands of the bubonic plague and driven by every surviving social hierarchy to bring Christianity to the rest of the world at sword point, it turned its sophisticated trade networks toward new markets and greater profits. Over the next several centuries it would proceed to enslave, kill, displace, or dominate most of the rest of the world. By 1900, Europe claimed power over most of the Americas, over 90 percent of Africa, over half of Asia, and nearly all of Australia and Polynesia.

Nowhere was this agenda more evident than in the Americas, where hundreds of indigenous nations—and most of the tens of millions of people who populated them—were wiped out by European colonists. To fully exploit the agricultural and mineral potential of this new world, the Europeans forcibly transported more than twelve million Africans across the Atlantic Ocean to assume new identities as slaves. Millions died in transit. Those who survived the journey but were unwilling to spend the rest of their lives working in the bondage of slavery, an ocean away from their homes and families, were executed.

EXPLORERS AND CONQUISTADORS

Spain of 1492 was a land dominated by material success, religious fervor, and a deep suspicion toward outsiders. Queen Isabella of Castile (1451–1504) and King Ferdinand II of Aragon (1452–1516) had recently presided over the Christian reconquest of al-Andalus, Muslim Spain, and—in direct violation of the peace treaty that gave them power over the Iberian Peninsula to begin with—had replaced its relatively tolerant and multicultural government with something decidedly less tolerant and decidedly less multicultural. So the idea of sailing west to find a backdoor to Asia, allowing the Spanish monarchy to forcibly spread its theology to new victims and dramatically cut down on trade-route lag time in the process, seemed appealing.

That's where the Italian explorer Christopher Columbus (1451–1506) comes in. Contrary to what you may have heard, he wasn't the first guy to believe the world was round (that belief had been relatively common since at least the time of the ancient Greeks), and he wasn't the first to suggest that you could take advantage of Earth's roundness to sail west to Asia. What made him stand out, instead, was something he got *wrong*: he believed the world was significantly smaller than it is and that a backdoor to Asia would be easier to find than any of his contemporaries had guessed. Isabella and Ferdinand granted him both funding and a royal charter and he, in what would be widely recognized both in 1492 and today as an act of lunacy, proceeded to sail west to Japan. From Spain.

Columbus's discovery of the island of Hispaniola, off the coast of the Americas, changed everything. It didn't change everything for him—he went to his grave still believing that he'd discovered the East Indies, proof that, as the Disney song goes, it really *is* a small world after all—but other explorers soon realized that there was another continent in play. An Italian mapmaker who most decisively made this argument also gave the new continent its name: Amerigo Vespucci (1454–1512), who drew the earliest known maps of the land, called it America.

Over the next several centuries, Spanish, French, and English explorers would set up shop in America. The most militarily aggressive of the three was, unsurprisingly, the Spanish. The rulers of Spain saw the New World as an opportunity to extend their divinely sanctioned Christian reconquest much farther west than anyone could have dreamed. They sent out conquistadors to stake claim to their own feudal *encomiendas* ("commendations"), which were forced labor camps stocked with natives who could be sent to work on mines and agricultural plantations. That's how the largest surviving precolonial Latin American civilizations, such as the Mayans and the Aztecs, were largely driven to extinction. Between the wars and the spread of European diseases, the famine and the displacements, European colonial empires and the independent states that branched off from them completed the most successful large-scale program of genocide in human history. We don't know for sure just how many natives of the

Americas died as a result of colonization—and we'll probably never know—but most credible estimates range in the tens of millions.

Who Was the Real-Life Pocahontas?

Although there was a historical Pocahontas (1596–1617), her life bore little resemblance to the Disney account.

Born Princess Matoaka of the Tsenacommacah tribal confederacy in Virginia, she was married twice—first as a teenager to a tribal warrior Kocoum (who died at the hands of the British army), and later to tobacco mogul John Rolfe (1585–1622).

Matoaka had become something of a celebrity in Britain after marrying Rolfe and taking on the name Rebecca. She died in transit under mysterious circumstances after insisting on sailing across the Atlantic to visit her estranged family in Virginia. She never married, and probably never even befriended, Admiral John Smith (1580–1631). Smith nonetheless claimed in his 1624 memoir that they knew each other well and that she had saved his life on multiple occasions, giving birth to the folk legend of Pocahontas. His story appears to have been completely fabricated. She would have been only ten years old at the time Smith visited the Tsenacommacah, and his dramatic account of events directly contradicts other records from the period.

THE TRANS-ATLANTIC SLAVE TRADE IN THE AMERICAS

The amount of territory in the Americas was so vast by European standards, and so relatively unexploited, that Europeans had no concept of how much labor it would take to monetize it. The whole of Europe is only 3.9 million square miles, and these empires had been fighting over little pieces of it for thousands of years. North and South America combined are 16.3 million square miles—more than four times as big, even if you don't count the islands—and they hadn't even begun to bleed it dry yet.

European colonial authorities tried capturing indigenous inhabitants and forcing them to work, and they tried bringing over indentured servants from Europe, but this wasn't enough to possess all the available resources to satisfy their greed. And so they turned to West Africa, stealing millions of indigenous inhabitants from yet another continent to serve as slave labor in the Americas.

1502
Juan de Córdoba, a silversmith and personal friend of Columbus, sends several of his African slaves to the Americas to serve as laborers.

1517
An estimated fifteen thousand West Africans are shipped by Portuguese slavers to labor in the mines and plantations of Spanish colonial America.

1619
The first twenty African slaves arrive in the English colony of Jamestown, Virginia, beginning the English colonial North American slave trade that would become the US slave trade.

1787
The Constitution of the newly independent United States does not prohibit slavery, but the government calls for an end to the import of slaves in 1808.

1808

The United States, which has by this point transitioned over to the forced breeding of African Americans as slaves, enacts its ban on further slave imports.

1811

All Spanish colonies in the Americas, except for Cuba, ban slavery.

1865

At the end of the American Civil War, the Thirteenth Amendment to the US Constitution—formally banning chattel slavery—is ratified.

The Invention of Race

Although skin color is as old as skin, and national origin as old as nations, race as we know it is a very new concept and was invented largely to justify unfair practices that were already underway, not as a scientific achievement. The first to outline anything resembling the racial categories we have now was the French doctor François Bernier (1620–1688), whose *A New Division of the Earth* (1684) reclassified humanity into "four or five Species or Races."

Over the next century or so, this concept was developed by other European thinkers into a "scientific" theory of race in which whites, or Caucasians, were generally singled out as the most advanced subspecies of humanity, justifying their exploitation of others. Proto-Nazi thinkers of the nineteenth century would later carry this idea to its conclusion, arguing that whites are a "master race" destined to conquer and subjugate the world.

The twentieth-century discovery of human DNA pointing to a common ancestor, and the subsequent discovery that the cosmetic racial differences identified by Bernier and his successors don't correspond neatly to racial categories and are in fact ephemeral in the grand scheme of things, has largely destroyed the idea of "race science." Today, race is generally considered a subject for social scientists, not biologists.

THE RISE OF PROTESTANT EUROPE

From the Tudors to the Thirty Years' War

"The longer the days are the farther off is the sun, and yet the more fierce. So it is with our love, for by absence we are parted, yet nevertheless it keeps its fervour, at least on my side, and I hope on yours also..."
—Henry VIII, in an undated letter to his mistress and future wife, Anne Boleyn, whom he would order beheaded several years later

---

As we discussed earlier, the medieval papacy was pretty solidly committed to creating a holy West—a kind of Christian caliphate—that would have operated under the indirect authority of a pope, with Christian emperors ruling over specific parts of Europe, but who answered to a higher power (or perhaps ideally, as in the case of Charlemagne, a new Holy Roman Emperor claiming global authority). It would be easy but excessively simplistic to dismiss this as a stereotypical evil scheme to take over the world. The truth is a lot more complicated. Medieval-era popes had a lot to worry about: the spread of Islam, still-surviving pagan customs, heresies, wars between Catholic states, and the corruption of clergy and monks who did terrible things in the name of the pope. And that's assuming the pope himself wasn't corrupt, which many medieval popes were. It was a tough job.

But it was about to get a whole lot tougher, thanks to reforms that were taking place within Christianity itself.

FIRST CAME THE TUDORS

If you've ever heard the story behind William Shakespeare's play *Richard III* (1592), you already have a pretty good idea of how the Tudors took control of the English monarchy. Recall that the brutal and unpopular King Richard III (1452–1485), who fought the upstart Henry Tudor (Henry VII, 1457–1509) at the Battle of Bosworth Field, fell to insurgent forces.

After Richard's long-lost remains were dug up in 2012 and successfully identified using DNA forensic testing, it was determined that he had died due to nine head wounds and was probably kneeling when he received the fatal blow—which means that the last words Shakespeare attributes to him ("A horse, a horse, my kingdom for a horse!") could plausibly have been his actual last words.

HENRY AND THE POPE

Henry Tudor's son, Henry VIII (1491–1547), reigned for thirty-eight years. While he did many notable things during this time, most people remember him primarily for one thing: marrying six different women and treating most of them really, really horribly.

Wife #1: Catherine of Aragon (1485–1536)

Henry's first—and longest (twenty-four years!)—marriage was to a woman he didn't have killed, presumably for sentimental reasons. After meeting the much younger future wife number two, Henry had his marriage to Catherine annulled against the pope's wishes. This broke off England's ties with the Roman Catholic Church (though in doing this Henry did not technically create the Church of England;

that happened decades later under Queen Elizabeth). Henry and Catherine had only one surviving child together: Mary I (1516–1558), who as queen would become known as "Bloody Mary." More on that later.

Wife #2: Anne Boleyn (1501–1536)

Henry's marriage to Boleyn lasted less than three years. Anne bore one child—the future Queen Elizabeth—but Henry wanted a male heir. When wife number three caught his eye, he had Anne beheaded for treason.

Wife #3: Jane Seymour (1508–1537)

Henry married Seymour only eleven days after having Boleyn decapitated. We'll never know how long his marriage to Seymour would have lasted if she hadn't died prematurely, but labor complications following the birth of future king Edward VI (1537–1553) ended her life only seventeen months after she'd become queen consort.

Wife #4: Anne of Cleves (1515–1557)

Anne got a pretty good deal: she and Henry were married for less than six months in 1540, and she survived for years afterward. Henry had the marriage annulled because they'd never actually had sex, and she lived out the rest of her natural life with the honorary title "The King's Beloved Sister."

Wife #5: Catherine Howard (1523–1542)

The middle-aged Henry had only been married to the teenaged Catherine for a year and a half when he had her (and her two alleged lovers) beheaded for adultery.

Wife #6: Catherine Parr (1512–1548)

This Catherine outlived Henry, her third husband, long enough to marry a fourth. It's tempting to say that Henry had finally met his match in Catherine Parr; one of his contemporaries, Lord Chancellor Thomas Wriothesley, remarked that she was "more agreeable to his heart" than the other five wives. But unlike Henry, she never had any of her husbands beheaded; although she was a four-time widow, each died of natural causes.

The Threefold Cord

While Henry VIII's break from the Roman Catholic Church is commonly associated with the Protestant Reformation, Anglican theologians tend to regard their tradition as something between Roman Catholicism and Protestantism, and not strictly as part of either. In contrast to Catholicism's focus on tradition and the Reformation's tendency toward *sola Scriptura* ("Scripture alone"), the Elizabethan theologian Richard Hooker (1554–1600) wrote of the "threefold cord not quickly broken" that undergirds the Anglican tradition: scripture, tradition, and reason. In Anglican and Episcopal confirmation classes, this is commonly referred to as Hooker's "three-legged stool" (a phrase that Hooker himself did not use).

THE ELIZABETHAN ERA

Henry VIII's raging libido and/or desire for a male heir did not, contrary to popular opinion, create the Church of England. Henry VIII considered himself a Roman Catholic in good standing until the day he died, and given the number of beheadings he was involved in it's unlikely that he encountered much argument. The Church of

England was actually created by Henry's daughter, Elizabeth, who was a product of his second marriage to Anne Boleyn. As we shall see, Elizabeth's path to the throne was not a straight line.

After Henry had Boleyn beheaded in 1536, he had their daughter, Elizabeth, declared illegitimate. This decision may have saved her life. It was not until Henry's death in 1547 that Elizabeth became a potential successor to the throne, as he identified her as third in line. First in line was the nine-year-old Edward VI, or rather the council of dukes who served as his regent until he reached adulthood. But Edward VI never assumed the throne, because he died suddenly at age fifteen. Second in line was Mary I, the very Catholic daughter of Henry's first wife, Catherine. Her nickname was Bloody Mary. And as you might have expected given that nickname, the reign of Mary I isn't fondly remembered—she attempted to convert England back to Catholicism by force, ordering Protestants executed often and in a very casual way. My own ancestor, Canterbury preacher Rowland Taylor (1510–1555), was among them, his death being fairly typical: he was accused of not being Catholic enough, whacked in the head with a halberd, and then burned at the stake. Bloody Mary didn't live much longer herself, passing away due to natural causes—probably ovarian cancer, but it's unlikely we'll ever know for sure—in 1558.

Shakespeare's Tongue

The most famous Elizabethan commoner was the poet and playwright William Shakespeare (1564–1616), who is more often than not described as the greatest writer in the history of the English language. While "greatest" is a matter of taste, the fact that he invented or popularized thousands of words, changing the language itself forever, is indisputable.

That cleared the way for Queen Elizabeth (1533–1603), who reigned for forty-four years—longer than any monarch had for centuries. One of her first acts was to create the Church of England. It's difficult to overstate just how drastic this change was. In 1557, advocating Anglicanism would get you burned at the stake; in 1559, it was effectively a job requirement for high-ranking clergy. This did not go over well, and Elizabeth had to spend much of the first few years of her tenure putting down violent rebellions. But in the end she got her way. Anglicanism, represented in the United States by the Episcopal Church, was the result. When she passed in 1603, Elizabeth, who never married, was buried alongside her sister, Bloody Mary—a touching gesture of reconciliation between Catholic and Anglican England, though perhaps not one with which Mary would have been entirely comfortable, all things considered.

THE GERMAN PROTESTANTS

While the theology of the German monk Martin Luther (1483–1546) would ultimately diverge from Roman Catholicism in some very important ways, it was the corruption of the church in the German states that ultimately drove him to split off from the tradition to which he had dedicated his life. Specifically, he was put off by a practice called the sale of indulgences—a scheme by which priests and monks of the day would allow people to literally buy their way, or (more often) buy their deceased friends' and family members' way, into heaven. The publication of Luther's *Ninety-Five Theses* (1517), and his translation of the Bible into ordinary German, had an explosive effect on the culture of Europe as a whole. The tradition he founded, Lutheranism, has eighty million adherents today.

But it was Luther's successful defiance of the Roman Catholic Church that brought the most change to Europe. After all, when the Czech theologian Jan Hus (1369–1415) had tried to do something similar a century earlier, local Catholic officials had him executed (though the small movement he founded, known as Hussitism, spread throughout central Europe and is still represented by several denominations to this day). Luther's rebellion was so public, and so audacious, he even took advantage of the new mass media of his time, the printing press, to spread his ideas. Once the pope himself was no longer the only representative of Western Christianity, a nation's religious affiliation became more of a bargaining chip, which in turn caused the institutional power of the Roman Catholic Church to be diminished. In response to this Protestant Reformation, over the next several centuries the Catholic Church itself would undergo an aggressive Counter-Reformation in an attempt to eliminate the corrupt practices, violent oppressive tactics, and secretive theological rationales that had sparked Luther's movement.

The Protestant Reformation is frequently blamed for the Thirty Years' War (1618–1648), a bloody and convoluted European war that involved dozens of small nations and cost more than eight million lives, and that blame is sort of warranted. The religious conflicts between Catholics and Protestants certainly started the war, but ambitious politicians and expansionist nations exploited these sentiments for very secular reasons. The more interesting question is whether the papacy would have been able to prevent the war in a united Catholic Europe. For all its faults, the papacy had historically been effective at preventing some conflicts between Catholic nations. And despite the papacy's significant loss of power, it remains, by and large, a force for peace to this day.

Sola Fide and Sola Scriptura

Two ideas that were of special importance to Luther were:

- *Sola fide* (Latin: "only faith"), the idea that salvation is attained through faith alone and not through works. Roman Catholicism has historically taught that good works are an essential product of faith, necessary for demonstrating that one is saved. Lutheranism teaches that good works, though present in the lives of faithful people, have nothing to do with salvation.
- *Sola Scriptura* (Latin: "only Scripture"), the idea that the Bible is the only source of divine revelation. Roman Catholicism has historically taught that divine revelation comes about in many different ways, including but not limited to the traditions of the Christian community itself.

THE AGE OF THE SAMURAI

The Warlords and Their Retainers

"All of man's work is a bloody business."
—Yamamoto Tsunetomo (1659–1719), samurai and author

If the older brother of Ashikaga Yoshimi (1439–1491) had just left him alone to live out his life as a Buddhist monk, as he'd originally planned, the history of Japan might have been very different. Unfortunately, Yoshimi's brother, Ashikaga Yoshimasa (1436–1490), was shogun (highest-ranking general) of Japan, had no children, and needed a designated heir for the sake of the kingdom. Yoshimi reluctantly accepted. Then Yoshimasa did the unthinkable: he had a son. And so he went to war against his own brother so that his son could inherit the empire. When his son died prematurely, he declared his nephew heir. And so on.

In the end, nobody was Yoshimasa's heir. By the time he died in 1490, he'd burned through all of his credibility and few people outside of his most loyal supporters even cared who he thought his successor ought to be. For over a century, local warlords battled over regional and national control until a clear victor emerged. This period, known in Japan as *Sengoku jidai* ("the period of warring provinces"), gave birth to the mythology surrounding a new kind of warrior: the warlord's noble knight-servant, the samurai.

WHEN WARRIORS RULED

Medieval Japan represents one of the few times and few places in the history of the world where military commanders, isolated to some extent from courtly manipulation and historic monarchial lines of succession, ruled the land. There was little dispute over who the emperor was, but imperial power wasn't the primary subject of dispute. It was the power of the shogun that really determined the trajectory of the country, and the shogun's identity was determined through war and subterfuge. It wasn't quite a battle royal—but it was much closer to being a battle royal than power struggles generally are.

Bushido

Just as knights were said to have lived by standards of chivalry, samurai lived by *bushi no michi* ("the way of the warrior") or, as some later came to describe it in the early twentieth century, *bushido* ("the warrior's path"). Among the most central texts of the bushi no michi tradition is the *Hagakure* ("hidden leaves"), a collection of aphorisms compiled by the samurai-turned-hermit Yamamoto Tsunetomo (1659–1719).

To the extent that the Sengoku jidai could be said to have had a winner at all, it was Tokugawa Ieyasu (1543–1616), who in 1603 united Japan under the leadership of his family and their loyal regional warlords. Japan would be ruled by Tokugawa and his successors until the Meiji Restoration of 1868, when the Emperor Meiji the Great (1852–1912) reasserted imperial power and brought Japan once more under the power of a united civilian government. While Japan would again come under the control of generals in the years leading up to World War I, and under imperial fascism during World War II, Meiji's tenure marked the end of the shogunate as the seat of Japanese political power.

THE FRENCH REVOLUTION AND ITS AFTERMATH

A Reign of Terror

"Citizens, did you want a revolution without revolution?"
—Maximilien Robespierre (1758–1794)

The French Revolution illustrates two basic political principles. The first is that if you're caught treating the majority of people badly in order to treat a small number of people very, very well, the consequences can be bloody. And the second is that if you overthrow an unjust system without a clear idea of what you're going to replace it with, things may ultimately change far less than you'd hoped—or change in a different way altogether.

The event that is commonly celebrated as the beginning of the French Revolution was the storming of the Bastille on July 14, 1789. Following escalating tensions between ordinary people and the upper classes (the nobility and the clergy), a crowd gathered outside the infamous Bastille Saint-Antoine, a prison and garrison. The governor of the Bastille called for a cease-fire, but when some protestors were shot by foot soldiers while attempting to enter, this was interpreted as a violation of the cease-fire. The protestors made it inside, despite as many as one hundred of them falling dead from the garrison's attacks. They captured the governor, decapitated him, and marched around with his head on a pole. For the more than two centuries since July 14 has been a national holiday in France—and a warning to tyrants around the world.

But the adoption by France's newly formed National Constituent Assembly of the *Declaration des droits de l'homme et du citoyen* ("Declaration of the Rights of Man and of the Citizen") six weeks later on August 26, 1789, might be just as relevant, at least to the broader history of the West. After all, the American and French Revolutions didn't just happen at roughly the same time; they fed into each other. The Marquis de Lafayette (1757–1834), who had famously fought for the winning side in America's War of Independence from England, played an equally prominent role in his own country's emerging revolution. Among his greatest achievements was principal authorship of this document, just as the American Founding Father James Madison's most preeminent achievement was authorship of the Bill of Rights. Both Lafayette and Madison had an inspiration behind the scenes: the Virginia plantation owner Thomas Jefferson (1743–1826), who advocated universal human rights with unprecedented effectiveness despite being, among other things, a slave owner. His words live on; every human rights document we rely on today, up to and including the Universal Declaration of Human Rights, bears some evidence of Jefferson's enduring influence.

THE DECLARATION OF THE RIGHTS OF MAN AND OF THE CITIZEN (1789)	
Article	Effect
I	Everyone is born with equal rights.
II	Governments exist to protect human rights.
III	Sovereignty comes from the nation, not the church or the monarchy.
IV	Everyone has a natural right to do anything that doesn't harm others.

V	Laws can only ban behavior that actually harms other people.
VI	All citizens have a right to participate in the democratic process.
VII	Nobody can be arrested or punished unless they actually break a law.
VIII	Arbitrary and excessive punishments are forbidden.
IX	Everyone should be presumed innocent until proven guilty.
X	Everyone has a right to hold unpopular opinions.
XI	Everyone has the right to free speech and freedom of the press.
XII	The military serves all citizens, not just the rulers.
XIII	Establishes an income tax.
XIV	All citizens have a say in how taxes are assessed and spent.
XV	All public officials should keep accurate and public records.
XVI	The Constitution depends on the rule of law and separation of powers.
XVII	Defines the individual right to property.

But the leaders of the French Revolution didn't live up to their own principles, executing King Louis XVI (1754–1793) for treason. The first vote came from the revolutionary Maximilien Robespierre (1758–1794), previously an outspoken opponent of capital punishment. "The sentiment that led me to call for the abolition of the death penalty," Robespierre famously said, "is the same that today forces me to demand that it be applied to the tyrant of my country."

Robespierre would go on to abolish due process for those accused of treason, executing over fifty thousand people—many of them without trial—in what has subsequently been remembered as the Reign of Terror. In July 1794, he was himself executed without trial.

Louis XVI was not France's last monarch, and Robespierre was not its last hypocritical reformer. But France had been so completely central to political life in Western Europe that the French Revolution, fractious and temporary though it was, changed the world. It was a reminder that, in the face of sufficient civilian unrest, even the oldest and most powerful empires on Earth can become vulnerable.

The Guillotine

Although we look back on the guillotine as a barbaric form of execution, being quickly decapitated in one stroke by a machine is a lot less drawn out and gruesome than being burned at the stake, drawn and quartered by horses, or slowly beaten to death on the breaking wheel. That efficiency was by design. The influential physician Joseph-Ignace Guillotin (1738–1814) was disgusted by the torture the French monarchy inflicted on capital defendants and demanded that the death penalty be abolished, or at least replaced by something less painful and more effective. Others responded by inventing a machine to efficiently decapitate those sentenced to death and, probably much to his horror, by naming it after him.

MANIFEST DESTINY AND THE AMERICAS

Democratic Hopes, Exploitative Greed

"After the wars and the killings had ended, when usually there survived only some boys, some women and children, these survivors were distributed among the Christians to be slaves."

—Bartolomé de las Casas (1484–1566)

By the time the English-American colonists revolted to create their own independent United States of America in 1776, Europeans had been present in the Americas for nearly three centuries. To say that their colonization efforts had been disruptive would be an understatement; they had functionally eradicated the indigenous American nations, directly or indirectly killing countless millions, and were in the process of importing over ten million slaves from Africa to serve as forced labor. Violence had already been established as a way of life; the fact that the European colonists themselves would ultimately end up at war with each other should be, in retrospect, no surprise.

That the heirs of this bloody business would ultimately establish a kind of liberal representative democracy, abolish chattel slavery after a civil war, and play a central role in establishing the international human rights instruments we rely on today should also be no surprise. As you have no doubt already observed so far in this book, humanity's greatest achievements and its greatest atrocities often come from the same people living in the same places with the same cultural values. And no political institution demonstrates this contradiction better than the American presidency.

Why Did America Declare Its Independence?

Thomas Jefferson (1743–1826) often framed the American Revolution as a conflict between individual rights and the monarchy. That was part of the story, but it wasn't the entire story. The five primary causes of the American Revolution are issues that observers of contemporary US politics will immediately recognize:

- **High taxes.** Britain had spent far more money protecting its North American colonial interests from other European powers than it had planned, and it tried to make up the difference by heavily taxing imported goods to the colonies.
- **Free trade.** The North American colonists tried to save money by importing goods from other European powers instead, but Britain wasn't having any of that.
- **Civil liberties.** British colonial officials had virtually unlimited search-and-seizure powers, which they used to try to find illegally smuggled goods.
- **Corruption.** These colonial officials often *kept* the aforementioned illegally smuggled goods, a process we now call civil forfeiture. Sometimes they kept goods that *weren't* illegally smuggled. Sometimes they took bribes. It was a messy and poorly supervised system.
- **Voter disenfranchisement.** The British government used flimsy and unconvincing excuses to deprive American colonists of their seats in Parliament, preventing them from being able to vote on issues like, say, tax policy, free trade, civil liberties, and corruption.

TWO MEN NAMED ANDREW

We tend to look at the postcolonial history of the Americas as if European colonists arrived on unsettled continents and worked the land themselves. But that wasn't what happened: they conquered occupied continents and then brought slaves over to build an economy for them. The colonization of the Americas centered on, and would not have been possible without, the conquest of its indigenous inhabitants. The North American economy that grew out of that process, whose taxation ultimately provoked the American Revolution, was directly supported by slavery. The often-dismissed "politically correct" questions of how American Indians and African-American slaves were treated by European colonists and their descendants are actually the most central questions in American history, and historians increasingly recognize them as such. Two presidents named Andrew were particularly influential in these areas—and not in a positive way.

Andrew Jackson (1767–1845)

Jackson took office as the seventh US president in 1829. He was a war hero, and you can get away with a lot if you're a war hero. Specifically, he was the major-general who led the badly outnumbered US soldiers to victory in the Battle of New Orleans, the last battle of the War of 1812. (A peace treaty had technically been signed prior to the Battle of New Orleans, unbeknownst to both sides.)

But most of Jackson's military experience involved taking land away from American Indian tribes, most notably the Creek and the Seminole, and he carried this trend even further during his presidency. After signing the Indian Removal Act in 1830, he forcibly drove American Indians out of the southeastern United States and into the western territories, killing thousands in the process, as part of a series of forced marches described by one of its Choctaw victims as "a trail of tears and death."

Jackson's record on slavery was nearly as bad. He entered office as the most prolific slave owner in Tennessee, and advocated slavery throughout both of his terms. In 1835, he even went so far as to ban the distribution by mail of antislavery writings in the South, giving postmasters in the region permission to censor content that was not fully supportive of the institution of slavery. Partly as a result of Jackson's influence, the Democratic Party remained proslavery until after the American Civil War.

Andrew Johnson (1808–1875)

You might expect the vice president who served under Abraham Lincoln (1809–1865) to be relatively supportive of African-American civil rights, but you'd be wrong. Johnson, a staunch Southern Democrat, represented the slavery-friendly half of a Lincoln "unity ticket" that was intended to help retain the support of Southerners who supported slavery but opposed the Confederacy.

After Lincoln was assassinated, Johnson did everything he could to prevent former slaves from being able to participate fully as citizens—unsuccessfully attempting to block passage and ratification of the Fourteenth Amendment (which gave citizenship to former slaves), supporting early Jim Crow legislation intended to deprive African Americans of civil rights, and providing cover for violent white supremacist groups that emerged in the aftermath of the American Civil War. He wasn't any kinder to American Indians, sending the US Army after any American Indian tribes that objected to being displaced to make room for the Pacific Railroad.

All told, Johnson's values—like those of so many early US leaders—were explicitly and unapologetically prejudiced. "This is a country for white men," Johnson wrote in a letter to the governor of Missouri, "and by God, as long as I am president, it shall be a government of white men." Johnson was unpopular, ultimately impeached (but acquitted), and did not seek another term. But his influence—and that of Jackson before him—would linger in the Democratic Party for a century to come. When Johnson's successor Horatio Seymour ran for president in 1868, he did so under a chilling ten-word slogan: "This is a white man's country. Let white men rule." And for most of the history of the United States, and the history of the colonial Americas before it, they brutally did just that.

KEY DOCUMENT: THE BILL OF RIGHTS (FINAL 1791 VERSION)

The US Constitution was ratified in 1787, but some dissenters asked a fairly reasonable question: why didn't it come with a bill of rights? Even the English government, the colonial government against which the Founding Fathers rebelled, had committed to one in 1689. The answer came on June 8, 1789, when James Madison (1751–1836), goaded by letters from Declaration of Independence author Thomas Jefferson in France, proposed an early draft of the series of civil liberties protections that we now know as the Bill of Rights. Its function was largely symbolic until 1925, when the US Supreme Court ruled in *Gitlow v. New York* that the Bill of Rights applied to both federal and state law.

THE US BILL OF RIGHTS (RATIFIED 1791 VERSION)	
Amendment	Rights Protected
I	Freedom of religion, speech, assembly, and journalism.
II	The right to bear arms as part of "a well-regulated militia."
III	The right to turn away soldiers who want to stay at your house without permission.
IV	The right to privacy, with exceptions.
V	The right to binding jury trials, the right to property, and the right to remain silent.
VI	The right to a fair trial.
VII	The right to jury trials in most civil cases, and the authority of trial courts.
VIII	Freedom from cruel, unusual, and excessive punishments.
IX	All rights not specified are reserved by the people.
X	The federal government doesn't have any powers it doesn't specifically claim.

EUROPE IN THE AGE OF NAPOLEON

The Devil's Favorite

"I have made all the calculations; fate will do the rest."
—Napoleon Bonaparte (1769–1821)

We all define greatness in different ways. Historians of earlier generations often had an idea of military greatness, of men (invariably men) who distinguished themselves by conquest. And that story of greatness was often ultimately the story of three men: Alexander the Great, Julius Caesar, and Napoleon, who was called "the devil's favourite" by the terrorized British military. Historical thinking has evolved, and we now have come to believe (as claimed by Yoda, from the Star Wars series) that "wars [do] not make one great." As a result, we're left with a harder question: once you take away the conquests, is there anything left of these men that we should think of as remarkable?

In the case of Napoleon, there just might be. He stands apart from the vast majority of the world's conquerors in that he actually seems to have had some coherent idea of what he wanted to do with the world once he took it over. If you're living in the industrialized West, you're likely to encounter bits of Napoleon's legacy in your everyday life.

FRANCE'S CAESAR

Napoleon rose to imperial power in much the same way Julius Caesar did: by achieving astonishing success as a military leader, and then using his subsequent popularity to disrupt a tired and unpopular civilian political system. By 1804, General Napoleon had become Emperor Napoleon—though his most successful days as a military leader were ahead of him. Over the next eight years he conquered nearly all of continental Western Europe in the name of France, building an empire that—although not among the largest in history—controlled a disproportionate amount of the world's trade and economic resources.

One of the lasting elements of Napoleon's legacy was the legal code that bore his name. This most ambitious systematic attempt to create a universal Western legal code since ancient Rome has had a profound structural influence on countless legal codes throughout the world, ranging from the Middle East to Poland to the US state of Louisiana. The Napoleonic division of law into the four categories of persons, property, acquisition of property, and civil procedure still stands to this day, even in many unrelated legal codes.

But it was all downhill for Napoleon after 1812, when he invaded Russia. His troops advanced toward Moscow, and the Russians fell back before them, burning crops and leveling houses. Although the emperor captured Russia's capital city, he didn't know what to do with it. The largely wooden city caught fire and burned, depriving the French soldiers of food and shelter. The Russian armies were still intact. After five weeks, Napoleon's Grand Army began its retreat. Caught by the Russian winter, which found them woefully unprepared, the soldiers stumbled along on frostbitten feet. Many collapsed and never arose. The army melted away, and Napoleon reached France with only a fraction of it still battle ready.

Forced from the government, he was sent into exile on the island of Elba. He escaped in 1814 and made his way back to France, where he raised an army. But he met his waterloo in June 1815 at, well, the Battle of Waterloo. Although he had already survived multiple defeats and multiple successful challenges to his imperial authority, he was captured and exiled to the remote island of St. Helena, more than a thousand miles from the nearest shore. There he lived out the remainder of his life before dying in 1821.

The Story of Margarine

You might have heard that Napoleon was responsible for the invention of margarine. That's sort of true; it was actually his less renowned nephew, Napoleon III (1808–1873), who gave chemist Hippolyte Mége-Mouriés (1817–1880) 12,000 francs, or a little over $150,000 in today's currency, for discovering the inexpensive butter substitute.

FROM BISMARCK TO THE WEIMAR REPUBLIC

Germany in the Gilded Age

"A statesman cannot create anything himself. He must wait and listen until he hears the steps of God sounding through events; then leap up and grasp the hem of his garment."

—Otto von Bismarck (1815–1898)

We justifiably think of Germany as a nation that has always been one country and, at most, two. But the working definition of Germany has changed dramatically over the centuries, and we owe the existence of what we currently think of as Germany to a series of skirmishes, diplomatic scandals, and political failures.

At the time the brilliantly diabolical Otto von Bismarck (1815–1898) first came on the national scene in 1866, he was a prominent Prussian legislator and diplomat who had risen to become the king's right-hand man. Prussia was the largest and most populous of the North German Confederation's twenty-two states, and through a series of relatively short-term, manageable wars—with Denmark, Austria, and France—Bismarck successfully created the need for a united Germany to deal with future military threats. Bismarck's king, Kaiser Wilhelm I (1797-1888), in turn became the first German emperor. But don't put too much stock into that title—there were only three.

The third and final German emperor, Kaiser Wilhelm II (1859–1941), achieved global notoriety as the aggressive leader of a united Germany during World War I. Upon Germany's defeat, Wilhelm became extremely unpopular and ultimately abdicated during the German Revolution of 1918. The government that replaced him, a constitutional democracy called the Weimar Republic (because its legislature met in the centrally located city of Weimar), seemed promising at first. But hobbled by the unfavorable treaty terms imposed on Germany after the war, the center-left parliamentary democracy proved so unpopular among both left-wing socialists and right-wing nationalists that the Nazi Party was able to gain a foothold, and had functionally achieved full control of the country by the end of the 1930s. Wilhelm II himself lived long enough to see the beginning of World War II, but not the end.

Pickelhelm

The famous German spiked helmets, called *pickelhelms* or *pickelhauben*, were distinctive but useless in combat. The spikes were generally dull, felt-covered, and, by the end of the nineteenth century, removable.

The history of Germany in the recent century has focused, understandably, on the horrors of Nazi Germany itself. But even in the decades before World War II, its history is instructive. Bismarck's success in nation building teaches us of the power that an elective war can give a leader, while Wilhelm II's failures tell us of the power that such a war can take away. The fall of the short-lived Weimar Republic, and the subsequent rise of Nazi power, tells us that there is a danger to whittling down the power of our institutions when we cannot yet foresee what will replace them.

THE STORY OF THE OTTOMAN EMPIRE

The Imperial Gate

"Men, I am not ordering you to attack. I am ordering you to die."
—Mustafa Kemal Atatürk (1881–1938), at the Battle of Gallipoli in 1915

The nation we think of as Turkey is, at the same time, heir to both the Byzantine Empire and the earliest Islamic caliphates. It is an autocracy with a democratic history, a secular nation with a fundamentalist history, an independent country of the modern world and the seat of ancient empires. And it became the country it is today through a series of improbable losses, atrocities, and progressive reforms.

At its largest in 1683, the Ottoman Empire controlled more than two million square miles, about half the size of Europe as a whole, stretching out from Algeria in the west to Mesopotamia in the east, from the Ukraine in the north to Mecca in the south. It controlled two-thirds of the Mediterranean coastline in every direction and functionally controlled the Mediterranean itself, with a powerful navy that rivaled those of the Western European powers. It was the most powerful Muslim nation on Earth and, after the fall of al-Andalus, the only powerful Islamic presence in Europe.

But by the mid-nineteenth century, the Ottoman Empire had shrunk considerably and struggled under economic stress and social change. Tsar Nicholas I (1796–1855), ruler of Russia, feared the destabilizing effect the collapse of his western neighbor might have. Of the Ottoman Empire, he said in 1853:

> "Turkey seems to be falling to pieces. The fall will be a great misfortune…We have a sick man on our hands, a man gravely ill. It will be a great misfortune if one of these days he slips through our hands, especially before the necessary arrangements are made."

But the empire survived another seven decades, transitioning partially to a democratic system after the Young Turk Revolution of 1908 and entirely to a secular democratic system after the Turkish War of Independence in 1923. Between those two dates lie modern Turkey's darkest moments: its perpetration of the genocide against the country's Armenian population, and its crushing defeat in World War I.

Ottomans

The word *Ottoman* lives on in English through our use of ottomans, padded seats that have no arms or backs and are often used as footrests. This style of furniture, which became popular elsewhere in Europe in the late eighteenth century, did originate in the Ottoman Empire, where people often sat or reclined on cushions that rested on large, elevated platforms. The Ottoman Empire also invented another, better-known piece of furniture that became popular in the West: the sofa, from the Arabic *suffa* ("bench").

Today, Turkey remains a major European power—a complex, diverse nation that bridges central Europe, Asia, the Mediterranean, and the Middle East. But under the rule of the increasingly autocratic president Recep Tayyip Erdogan (1954–), its future as a democracy is unclear.

THE INDUSTRIALIZATION OF THE WEST

Coal and Steel

"Civilization advances by extending the number of important operations
which we can perform without thinking of them."
—Alfred North Whitehead (1861–1947), mathematician and philosopher

From a distance, the entire history of humanity can be reasonably broken down into three stages: the hunter-gatherer period, the stable agriculture period, and the industrial period. Most of what we think of as modern, contemporary, and "developed" is a product of the Industrial Revolution. We would find it difficult to adapt to the world that preceded it, and the people who lived in that world might have found it even harder to adapt to the world that was to come, or even imagine it. As technology made it possible to pursue increasingly fast and increasingly ambitious production goals, the financial powers of the world began to exploit coal, metals, and human bodies on an unprecedented scale.

Industrialization had many unintended consequences, among them the exacerbation of an existing technology gap that gave European colonial armies advantages over indigenous armies they sought to overpower. As traditional societies armed with bows and spears bravely faced down hordes of well-organized invaders armed with cannons and rifles, the fight between the empires of the world and their future subjects became less and less fair.

Labor Unions

Although most of today's politicians in the western hemisphere tend to dismiss labor unions and disparage worker strikes, it was unions—and the threat of strikes—that gave us the minimum wage, the five-day/forty-hour workweek, overtime pay, holidays, family and sick leave, employee benefits, safety inspections, an end to forced child labor, and many other things. Without labor unions, industrialization could easily have created a feudal society.

TIMELINE OF KEY INVENTIONS

MAJOR INVENTIONS OF THE INDUSTRIAL ERA	
Technology	Year Invented
Practical steam engine	1712
Flying shuttle (weaver's tool)	1733
Refrigeration	1755
Spinning jenny (weaver's tool)	1764
Carbonated water	1767
Steam-driven passenger vehicle	1769
Weighting scale	1770
Air compressor	1776
Steamboat	1783
Thresher	1786
Power loom	1789
Cotton gin	1793
Hydraulic press	1795
Vaccine	1798
Papermaking machine	1799

Electrical battery	1800
Steam locomotive	1804
General anesthesia	1804
Canned food	1810
Electric telegraph	1816
Photography	1827
Lawnmower	1830
Steam shovel	1839
Synthetic fertilizer	1842
Reinforced concrete	1853
Color photography	1855
Rechargeable batteries	1859
Synthetic plastic	1862
Pasteurization	1864
Dynamite	1867
Stainless steel	1872
Metal detector	1874
Telephone	1876
Lightbulb	1879
Bicycle	1885
Gas-powered automobile	1886
Ballpoint pen	1888
Zipper	1891
Radio	1895
X-ray machine	1895
Vacuum cleaner	1901
Motorized aircraft	1903
Television	1909
Tank	1915

FEMINISM'S FIRST WAVE

Women and the Global Order

"The nearer society approaches to divine order, the less separation will there be in the characters, duties, and pursuits of men and women. Women will not become less gentle and graceful, but men will become more so."

—Lydia Maria Child (1802–1880)

Part of the reason you don't hear more about the lives of specific women over the bulk of human history is because so much of that information has been lost or destroyed or never recorded. While we have some impressive testimonies written by women at various points in history, they're more the exception than the rule. More often we're forced to speculate, drawing on archaeology and bits of evidence here and there to figure out how women might have lived in a given place at a given time. But to whatever extent we have first-hand documentary testimony telling anyone's story, it has primarily told the stories of men.

This is no accident. Sexism is among the most ancient and fundamental forms of prejudice, and it has irreparably smudged the historical record. But women in all societies, in countless ways, have fruitfully resisted this erasure. In the West, in the tradition we now call first-wave feminism, the story of the vindication of the rights of women began as a challenge to Enlightenment philosophies of the vindication of the rights of men—philosophies that, like so many before them, left out half of humanity.

FROM THEORY TO SUFFRAGE

It is folly to declare any date as being the year gender liberation started, because in a sense the genesis of this liberation is at least as old as gender itself. The ancient Sumerians, whose 4,000-year-old documents are the oldest we have, embraced a flexible definition of gender that allowed a woman named Kubaba to be king and numerous men to be priestesses of the goddess Ishtar. The female pharaoh Hatshepsut (1507–1458 B.C.E.) not only ruled over Egypt for two decades at the height of the Eighteenth Dynasty, but she was also frequently depicted in sculpture with a beard. Almost every kingdom that lasted for any significant period of time had queens as well as kings, and some of the most formidable armies of the ancient world—those of the Scythians, Parthians, and even the Mongols—had female archers whose victims were just as dead as those slain by any man. Until the European colonial era, most societies had more than two genders—and fairly sophisticated ideas of what gender meant. Chinese culture, for example, treated gender as a social construct thousands of years before Western sociologists reached that conclusion.

But there's something specific and peculiar about the Western tradition we call feminism. As a response to a specific oppressive gender structure, and one that had spread throughout the world due to colonialism, first-wave feminism existed in a specific place and time as an attempt to expand the values of the Enlightenment. Seventeenth- and eighteenth-century European philosophers helped transform the Western legal tradition when they began to emphasize natural rights and prioritize reason over tradition, but they did not generally advocate for the natural rights of women, as they advocated those of men. Simply put, Enlightenment thinkers were mostly white men who treated reason as a white male attribute and tended not to trust people who weren't white men to wield its power. And to the extent that this allowed white men to act as if only they could reason gave them a pretense to allow only white men to vote in the democracies that their ideas inspired.

The first major work of feminist philosophy as such was *A Vindication of the Rights of Woman* (1792), written by the philosopher Mary Wollstonecraft (1759–1797); her daughter Mary Wollstonecraft Shelley would later become more famous for writing the first modern sci-fi novel, *Frankenstein* (1818). But during her time the elder Wollstonecraft was a celebrity in her own right. During the great debate between the Irish statesman Edmund Burke and the American pamphleteer Thomas Paine over the French Revolution, Wollstonecraft initially weighed in on Paine's side—and in defense of natural rights—with her *A Vindication of the Rights of Men* (1790), but she soon realized that the conversation between these men left out half the human race.

Wollstonecraft was not the only thinker to have entertained these ideas. A young Abigail Adams (1744–1818), wife of American Founding Father John Adams (1735–1826), wrote to her husband in 1776 cautioning him to "remember the ladies," who "will not hold ourselves bound by any Laws in which we have no voice, or Representation." Her husband replied in a patronizing and dismissive way, as most American and European politicians would for a century and a half to come.

The US and European women's suffrage movement gathered a full head of steam at the Seneca Falls Convention of July 1848, where hundreds of activists assembled to demand voting rights. The Declaration of Sentiments and Resolutions from this convention, both principally authored by Elizabeth Cady Stanton (1815–1902), helped animate and inspire seven decades of suffragist activism.

Both the United States and Britain would ultimately grant women as a class the right to vote, the United States with the Nineteenth Amendment of 1920 and Britain with the Representation of the People Act of 1928, though women who weren't white were still subjected to racist voter suppression laws in the United States, and especially in the American South.

Gender and Its Artifacts

Transgender rights are often presented by the media as the new frontier of civil rights activism, and transgender people as a community that didn't even exist until recent decades. History tells a more complicated story: that for as long as gender has existed, there has been gender nonconformity and gender fluidity.

That's not speculation; it's in the extant texts. More than 4,000 years ago, in documents that are among the oldest ever written, Sumerian scribes wrote of spear-wielding priests of Inanna who were born girls but grew up to become men, and sacred dancers who were born boys but grew up to become women. The Egyptian pharaoh Hatshepsut was portrayed as feminine in some drawings, shirtless and bearded in others.

Ancient Hindu texts speak of the *napumsa* or *tritiya-prakriti*, people who are neither male nor female. Ancient Jewish texts speak of the *tumtum*, individuals without a clear male or female identity. In the Americas, the Incans listened to the counsel of androgynous priests named *quariwarmi* while the North American Ojibwe had both the *ikwekaazo* ("men who live as women") and *ininiikaazo* ("women who live as men") and the Navajo had the double-gendered *nadleeh* (commonly translated as "Two-Spirit").

Everyone alive today, regardless of their personal identity, is contributing in some way to the story of gender. And as our vocabulary around gender expands, we will find in that new vocabulary both echoes of old identities and old ways of thinking and, perhaps, vague premonitions of a future we can't quite imagine yet.

IMPERIALISM AND THE MODERN WORLD

The Last Global Empires

"We are not interested in the possibilities of defeat; they do not exist."
—Queen Victoria of the United Kingdom (1819–1901)

One of the great myths of history is that Christopher Columbus discovered America. As he himself conceded, he didn't. Columbus merely discovered America for Europe, and in much the same way that Europe "discovered" most of the rest of the world: as farms, mines, and hunting grounds.

At the turn of the twentieth century, the existing great empires held almost unchallenged dominion over the world. Materially, this was an impressive achievement—but most of the nations exploited by these empires are still recovering both politically and economically, often placing them at strategic disadvantages that they might otherwise never have faced. The massive empires of Europe dug deep wounds into the world that still haven't healed, feeding conflicts that will probably outlive us all.

THE MAJOR PLAYERS OF THE IMPERIAL AGE

When the nineteenth century became the twentieth, the British Empire was without question the most powerful empire on Earth and the most powerful empire that had ever existed on Earth. Ruling over a quarter of the world's land, and spread throughout almost every time zone, presided over by the aging Queen Victoria, it could be said—and was often said—that the sun never set on the empire. No matter what time of day it was, there was some part of the British Empire where it was about noon, another where it was about midnight.

The Lion of Judah

Although most of Africa fell prey to European colonial powers during the late nineteenth and early twentieth centuries, Ethiopia was never conquered. This was in part due to the good fortune and ingenuity of the Ethiopian emperor Menelik II (1844–1913), who organized a powerful regional alliance to resist the Italian invaders. That alliance crushed the Italian army, functionally driving them out of the region, at the Battle of Adwa in 1896. Ethiopia was briefly occupied by Italian fascists during World War II, some forty years later. Despite many temporary occupations by Axis powers, Ethiopia's independence was restored in 1941. It remains independent to this day.

Britain was, of course, not the only significant world power. Russia under the tsars claimed about 15 percent of the world's territory, an empire roughly the same size as the USSR. China, always a force to be reckoned with, remained Asia's center of gravity. France, the Ottoman Empire, Portugal, and Spain, though not as powerful as they once were, still held considerable power and influence over the world. And the emerging nations of Japan and the United States had developed bold imperial ambitions, ambitions that would shape the course of the century to come.

But Britain of 1900 was a massive empire for the ages—larger than the Roman, larger than Persia or Alexandrian Greece, larger by far (it goes without saying) than any empire that has emerged or hoped to emerge in the century since. Even if the European Union were to formally become a single nation, encompassing all of Europe, it would still be less than a third the size of Britain in its prime.

IN THE TRENCHES

The War to End All Wars

"The lamps are going out all over Europe:
we shall not see them lit again in our lifetime."

—Edward Grey (1862–1933), British statesman

Calling World War I an unnecessary war is arguably redundant, since most wars are preventable. This was true for World War I: it wasn't an inevitable, unavoidable war. But when one looks at the global scale of this conflict, it's almost ridiculous to consider that it began with such an unlikely series of escalations and counter-escalations. Ultimately, over sixteen million people died because Austria-Hungary made unrealistic demands in its collective grief, because German leaders saw an opportunity for expansion, and—most of all—because of one troubled young assassin who could not have possibly anticipated how much damage he was about to do to the world.

IN THE TRENCHES

When the beloved young Austro-Hungarian heirs Archduke Franz Ferdinand and Duchess Sophie of Hohenberg visited Sarajevo in late June 1914, European diplomacy was already a little tense. Austria-Hungary had recently annexed the region from the Ottoman Empire, a decision that displeased Serbian nationalists who had hoped to add the city to the growing Serbian kingdom. The heirs' visit had been expected to smooth over some tensions between the leadership of Austria-Hungary and local officials, but in a matter of seconds Gavrilo Princip, an excited nineteen-year-old Serbian nationalist eager to prove himself, blew away the heirs—and, with them, any hope for peace.

Within a week of this assassination, Austria-Hungary formed a secret military alliance with Germany and privately made plans for war. The letter Austro-Hungarian officials sent to Serbia on July 23 made a series of demands that they knew would be impossible to satisfy, among them the freedom for Austro-Hungarian police to operate throughout the Serbian kingdom and arrest suspects at their own discretion—a clear violation of Serbia's sovereignty. Serbia sent a conciliatory reply five days later and suggested that further negotiation toward a mutually acceptable series of demands would be welcome, but that was not enough; Austria-Hungary declared war immediately.

For its part, Germany negotiated a secret alliance with the Ottoman Empire and decided to take advantage of the regional instability to negotiate a joint invasion of Russia. By the end of 1914, the conflict had escalated to become a true world war that would ultimately pit the Central Powers (led by Austria-Hungary, Germany, the Ottoman Empire, and Bulgaria) against the Allied Powers (led by Serbia, Russia, Britain, France, Italy, Japan, and Romania). The conflict in Europe was marked by long, protracted sieges that often included trench warfare, chemical weapons, large-scale artillery, and air combat. The most violent technologies the industrial age had to offer were let loose on Europe, leaving a generation of young men slaughtered, maimed, and broken.

It was a war that's remembered today as much for its battles as for its atrocities: Germany's decision to sink the world's largest civilian passenger ship, the RMS *Lusitania*, killing 1,198 people for no strategically defensible reason, is but one of many examples. This war is also remembered for both the aggressive continental aspirations of Germany, which would return in full force in World War II, and for the end of the Ottoman Empire—not just the way the war destroyed it, but the way it damned itself by using the war as cover to execute over 1.5 million civilians in the Armenian genocide.

This war also presaged far-flung alliances that would characterize all large-scale wars to follow. Indeed, the first to join the war in defense of Serbia and Russia were the old guard of Europe: France, Italy, Britain, and Romania. But Japan and the United States would soon assist the Allies, and South Africa the Central Powers, expanding the geography of the horror and lending a truly global scale to this conflict. This was mostly a European war, but it was never entirely a European war. The whole world was potentially at risk.

Mustard Gas

World War I had its share of new technological horrors. The worst of these was chemical warfare, which killed ninety thousand soldiers and incapacitated over a million more. The deadliest of these new weapons was dichlorodiethyl sulfide: mustard gas. Known for its yellow-brown color and pungent horseradish smell, mustard gas burned the eyes, skin, and lung tissue of its victims, covering them in agonizing pus-filled blisters. It was a terrible way to die, and even the survivors—who were often too badly injured to ever return to the battlefield—carried the scars and memories of their experiences with them for the rest of their lives.

When the Allies finally defeated the Central Powers on June 28, 1919—five years to the day after the assassination of Ferdinand and Sophie—the resulting Treaty of Versailles left Germany hobbled and humiliated. That, in turn, fomented a nationalist rage in Germany that would bring about a second, even more disastrous world war less than a generation later.

TRIUMPH OF THE BOLSHEVIKS

Tsar Wars

"A sledgehammer breaks glass, but forges steel."
—Leon Trotsky (1879–1940)

There was a great deal more going on in the Russian Revolution than the need to find a test case for Marxist political philosophy, but if that was the objective, the Bolsheviks would have been hard-pressed to find a more effective one. If ever a monarch deserved to get taken out in the woods and shot, the undeniably brutal and incompetent Tsar Nicholas II (1868–1918) was it. But the young revolutionaries would soon learn that cooking up a national government from scratch isn't easy to do, especially when you refuse to use any of the existing recipes.

The new Soviet Union was, almost overnight, one of the largest nations in human history. Its future would become one of brutal oppression, routine purges, unforgivable atrocities, and ideologically driven paranoia. But it would also sacrifice more lives than any other nation to stop Nazi Germany, and it survived a forty-year Cold War with the United States at the peak of the latter's power and influence. The fact that it accomplished these things on a massive scale under the banner of an untested political philosophy, the fact that it lasted seventy years in any form, is a testament to how badly the vanguards of the Soviet Union wanted their experiment to work.

KEY FIGURES IN EARLY
SOVIET HISTORY

The story of the Soviet Union was, like the story of all countries, ultimately the story of human beings. Here are a few who decided its trajectory:

Vladimir Lenin (1870–1924)

A century after his death the body of Lenin still lies perfectly preserved for public display—the only major Soviet leader to hold this distinction. (Stalin's body was displayed alongside Lenin's for eight years, then buried.) Lenin was the primary intellectual and political force behind the structure of the early Soviet Union, and is generally regarded as its founder.

Alexander Bogdanov (1873–1928)

A brilliant philosopher, medical researcher, sci-fi author, and close friend of Lenin, Bogdanov was instrumental in building the ideology of the Soviet Union but was effectively fired from its administrative ranks in 1922 for excessive freethinking. He is perhaps most famous today for his dubious belief that human life could be prolonged indefinitely using blood transfusions.

Leon Trotsky (1879–1940)

Trotsky was a central founder of the Soviet Union, creator of the Red Army, and served as a high-ranking official during its first decade. After a dispute within the leadership that resulted in the rise of Stalin, he was shut out of the upper echelon of Soviet leadership.

After Trotsky criticized the brutal excesses of Stalinist autocracy, Stalin had him assassinated.

Joseph Stalin (1878–1953)

Second only to Lenin, Stalin was the most significant figure in Soviet history. He ruled over the Soviet Union for thirty years.

Nikita Khrushchev (1894–1971)

Widely disparaged in the West due to his intimidating features, his harsh rhetoric, and his country's brutal suppression of political dissent, Khrushchev privately condemned Stalinist excesses and even attempted some modest humanitarian reforms. Communist hardliners removed him from office after less than a decade.

Karl Marx

Although the German-English revolutionary Karl Marx (1818–1883) is often thought of as an architect of Soviet ideology, he died a half-century too early to see his ideas put into practice on a full government scale. His focus was on the rights of working-class laborers, who were almost universally exploited during his lifetime and often encountered violence if they asked for better treatment. He also wrote extensively against slavery, which was a reality in the United States during much of his adult life.

THE THREE AGES OF MODERN CHINA

The Auspicious Cloud

"The Chinese people have only family and clan groups; there is no national spirit. Consequently, in spite of four hundred million people gathered together in one China, we are in fact but a sheet of loose sand...Our position is extremely perilous; if we do not earnestly promote nationalism and weld together our four hundred million into a strong nation, we face a tragedy—the loss of our country and the destruction of our race."
—Sun Yat-sen (1866–1925), president of the Republic of China

If any country inherits the superpower mantle abandoned by the United States and USSR following the Cold War, it will most likely be China. The most populous country on Earth, China is the emerging industrial capital of the world and by the year 2050 is likely to replace the United States as the seat of the world's largest economy. That's a remarkable achievement for a country that has been, for much of its recent history, impoverished, unstable, and riddled with large-scale ideological conflicts. No country changed more over the course of the twentieth century than China, and no country seems better positioned to influence the trajectory of the twenty-first.

CHINA IN TRANSITION

Outside of World War II, the two most significant events in Chinese history over the course of the twentieth century were the transition from the 244-year-old Qing dynasty to the nationalist Republic of China in 1912 and the transition from the Republic of China to the Communist People's Republic of China in 1949.

From Qing to the Republic

Before the twentieth century, China has historically alternated between division and unity under dynastic control. This changed with the Xinhai Revolution of 1912, when pro-democracy activists led by Sun Yat-sen overthrew the monarchs and established a democratic republic. This government asserted Chinese unity at a time when a profound external threat, the Empire of Japan, posed an existential challenge to the nation.

From the Republic to the People's Republic

Chinese Communists cooperated militarily with the nationalist government during World War II, but beginning in 1946 the promise of economic reform prompted a revolution. The People's Republic of China under Mao Tse-tung (1893–1976) took control of the mainland, with the Republic of China retreating to Taiwan, where it remains to this day.

Much like his Soviet predecessor Stalin, Mao attempted to implement his utopian vision with little concern for how it affected people in the short term. During what he called the Great Leap Forward of 1958 to 1962, Mao's attempts to industrialize the world's most populous country in less than five years led to the deaths of tens of millions of people. And despite his famous promise to "let a thousand flowers bloom," welcoming criticism, his Cultural Revolution, which lasted from 1966 until his death, amounted to a Communist answer to the Spanish Inquisition of the fifteenth century: an attempt to impose a single ideology on a diverse society by force. By the time Mao died in 1976, he had been directly or indirectly responsible for more than fifty million deaths—more than any single leader in history.

The Little Red Book

Mao Tse-tung's Little Red Book, officially published as *Quotations from Chairman Mao Tse-tung* (1964), features two hundred of his thoughts on various political issues. The most frequently quoted among them is his statement that declares, "Political power grows out of the barrel of a gun." This philosophy is an almost exact counterpoint to Gandhi's philosophy of *satyagraha*, which champions nonviolent political resistance.

THE TERRIFYING POWER OF STALINISM

Triumph of the Red Tsar

"He wants to turn the whole world upside down...I'll kill such a son with my
own hands; he's disgraced me."
—Besarion Jughashvili (1850–1909), father of Joseph Stalin

How far would you go to make the world run the way you wish it
did? For Soviet leader Joseph Stalin, there seemed to be no limit.
To serve his vision, he was willing to transform his country into
an oppressive police state, starve millions of children, and even
have his friends murdered. But he was also willing, once invaded,
to stop the fascists—even at the cost of as many as thirty million Soviet lives. Furthermore, during the first years of the Cold
War, he was committed to upholding Communist ideology in the
face of a prosperous and militarily powerful foe in the form of the
United States.

Stalin is a cautionary tale about how far politics, war, ideology, and ambition can take you. Does too much power erode your
humanity, or are the least human among us the best equipped to take
power? Once you've got the whole world in your hand, how long can
you resist the temptation to dig your fingers into it?

COLLECTIVISM AND PARANOIA

On paper, Communism is the Robin Hood of political ideologies: It purports to take from the rich and give to the poor. The whole idea of a Communist autocrat is hard to square with Karl Marx's original philosophy, set forth in *The Communist Manifesto* (1848), which sought to free the working class from both its public- and private-sector oppressors and create a new society grounded in universal human dignity. And the idea of a Communist autocrat killing thirty million people—many of them impoverished farmers who starved to death under utopian but heartlessly inflexible collectivization reform proposals of the 1930s—is a perversion of the concept. Stalin's constant censorship, show trials, imprisonments, and executions of his critics (or random officials he falsely imagined to be his critics) gradually made it difficult to associate the Soviet Union with *any* ideology outside of Stalin's personality cult. His personal need for approval and loyalty gradually conflicted with, and ultimately eclipsed, his commitment to Communist ideology.

"Tankies"

From the 1920s on, many US and European leftists saw hope in the bold Communist experiment. As Stalin's atrocities became more severe, however, it became increasingly hard to defend the Soviet implementation of Marxism. Those who chose to overlook or defend Stalinist human rights abuses in their defense of Soviet Communism were given the pejorative "tankies," so named after Stalin's tendency to suppress revolts using tanks.

But to their credit, later Soviet leaders did recognize this. Soon after taking office, Stalin's successor, Nikita Khrushchev, famously condemned Stalinist atrocities, and what he characterized as Stalin's cult of personality. And while leaders after Khrushchev did restore many of Stalin's repressive policies, they never gave him the reverence he demanded. Stalin was a dominating giant in life, but he was widely regarded as a national embarrassment after his death.

WORLD WAR II AND THE END OF PROGRESS

The Horror of Absolute War

"It is us today. It will be you tomorrow."
—Haile Selassie I (1892–1975), Ethiopian emperor in exile, after his country fell
to Italian fascists in 1936

War is very seldom a story of good versus evil, but World War II was a terrifying special case. It's difficult to construct an argument that would place the Allies and the aggressive and openly genocidal Axis Powers on the same moral footing, and anyone who tries is probably trying a bit too hard.

World War II, the largest and bloodiest war in human history, ended in a way that showed us both the seeds of our own potential destruction as a species (in the form of nuclear weapons) and the destruction of the human soul (in the form of the Holocaust). Before World War II, no matter how cynical a view one took of human nature, there was hope of progress. But the horrors of the war seemed to take aim at progress itself, and showed us that it has as much capacity for evil as it has for good.

ROME, BERLIN, AND TOKYO

The stakes of World War II were so high, and the war itself such a huge part of the twentieth century's mythology, that it's easy to forget how close the Axis Powers came to victory. Had Japan not brought the United States into the war by attacking Pearl Harbor, they would have had no rival in the naval Pacific theater; had Nazi Germany not brought the Soviet Union into the war with an unprovoked attack, they might have had the resources to hold continental Europe. We owe the survival of the global order as we know it to the hubris of dictators.

In the beginning came the betrayals. A disgruntled survivor of Germany's expansionist efforts during World War I, Adolf Hitler (1889–1945) blamed his nation's postwar economic and political difficulties on Jews, Communists, and any others he deemed its saboteurs. He was not, and did not aspire to be, rational in his approach to leadership; his fixation was on destiny, his own and Germany's. After losing a national election, then securing appointment as chancellor in 1933 anyway, he ruled over Nazi Germany for six years before shocking the world with the invasion of Poland in September 1939, the event that effectively started the war in Europe.

Compared to Benito Mussolini (1883–1945), the veteran fascist leader who came to power in Italy in 1922 and held it for nearly twenty years before revealing his ambitions, Hitler was a clumsy neophyte. Mussolini publicly promised to remain neutral in the great European war while privately strategizing with Hitler on the question of how and when he could most effectively break his promises to the rest of the continent. Mussolini saw his opportunity in June 1940 with the Nazi occupation of France.

In Japan, the Emperor Shōwa (1901–1989)—still generally known in the West by his given name, Hirohito—had reclaimed imperial power from military authorities in the late 1920s, and turned a predatory eye to China. His 1931 invasion of the mainland was ultimately followed by nearly four hundred large-scale chemical weapon attacks and numerous other atrocities (most notable among them being the Rape of Nanking in December 1937, which claimed the lives of more than three hundred thousand Chinese civilians). When he signed the Tripartite Pact with Germany and Italy in September 1940, forming the Axis Powers, it was without question an alliance among three fascist dictators who had no respect for the concept of human rights or the safety of civilians—their own, or those of their enemies.

In the end, the Axis Powers lost to the Allies after a series of blunders. The largest for Japan was the invasion of Pearl Harbor in December 1941, an event that gave US leaders pretext to enter the war and turn its considerable industrial might toward destroying the Japanese Navy's dominance of the Pacific. Only seven months later, Japan's decisive loss at the Battle of Midway forced it into a costly and unsustainable defensive posture—one that it abandoned only after the US became the first and only nation in history to use nuclear weapons in combat in August 1945, killing more than fifteen hundred thousand civilians during the bombing of Hiroshima and Nagasaki.

Nazi Germany's major error came sooner and in a much bloodier fashion. When Hitler invaded the Soviet Union in June 1941, he both violated a binding nonaggression pact and picked a fight with the world's largest army. The vast majority of military casualties throughout the war were German and Soviet, and the conflict between these two massive armies left Nazi Germany unable to maintain its occupation of France, much less expand westward. Both Hitler and Mussolini died in April 1945—Hitler at his own hands, Mussolini at the hands of enraged Italian civilians—and Allied victory in Europe came a month later.

Entire volumes could be, and have been, written about the military history of World War II; there's no way to convey the full scope of the war, or the dramatic arc of its battles, here. But the social and political consequences of this conflict were no less epochal; the war's scale prompted unprecedented multilateral peace and human rights agreements, while its atrocities seemed to destroy the very notion of human progress. The worst of these was the Holocaust, the planned extermination by Adolf Hitler of all European Jews; out of the continent's total prewar Jewish population of nine million, two-thirds—six million—were killed. The methods the Nazis and their allies used were as gruesome as they were systematic, and the scale was horrific. The Holocaust had other victims too—more than one hundred thousand Romani, more than two hundred thousand people with disabilities, ten thousand lesbians and gay men, and any residents of Germany or the occupied territories who resisted. All told, an estimated eleven million civilians perished by Hitler's command.

The Manhattan Project

Although the top-secret Manhattan Project (founded in 1942) was ultimately responsible for the design of the atomic bombs that would destroy Hiroshima and Nagasaki in August 1945, this US program was built on prior German, British, and Canadian research. It relied especially on that of the top-secret Tube Alloys program—a British project that discovered that a bomb could be built using achievable amounts of enriched uranium.

ZIONISM AND ISRAELI INDEPENDENCE

A Jewish Nation in the Holy Land

"According to the ideas current among Zionists today, all that is needed is to establish the conditions for a normal national life, and everything will come of itself. This is a fatal error."

—Martin Buber (1878–1965), philosopher

Decades before the Holocaust seemed even a distant possibility, the founding Reconstructionist rabbi Mordecai Kaplan (1881–1983) dedicated his life to seeing the Jewish people through a century that seemed likely to eliminate their faith and culture. Among the ideas he entertained, but did not focus on, was Zionism—a longstanding fringe political movement to create a new Jewish Holy Land in what was once called Israel but had long since operated under Ottoman, and then British, occupation.

After the end of World War II, the nations of the West elected to make the dream of Zionism a reality and create a new Israel in the British territory of Palestine. But the presence of a new Western-backed country in the region did not always sit well, especially among the native Palestinians who found themselves suddenly under the jurisdiction of a foreign state.

PEACE ON EARTH

People tend to talk about Israel-Palestine within the context of "peace in the Middle East," because things have been kind of a mess in the region since 1948. These conflicts reach back in time further than that, really, as European control over the Middle East, parallel to and followed by dueling US and Soviet Cold War control over the Middle East, have made a powder keg out of the region. Western powers have treated the Levant in particular—the countries on the east coast of the Mediterranean—as if they were absentee landlords. The sloppy way Britain handled the rollout of Israel after World War II is a case in point.

Shoah

Although English-speaking writers began widely using the term *Holocaust* in the 1950s, it was initially more widely known within the Jewish community as the *Shoah* or *Ha-Shoah* (Hebrew: "the calamity"), and this term is still widely used to this day.

Not that the Jewish immigrants who resettled in Israel hadn't also been profoundly victimized by the West, having been targeted— and having had over a third of their global population slaughtered— by Nazi Germany. Moreover, the indigenous residents of the Middle East were caught up in the cross fire of World War II: the Axis and Allied Powers fought brutally over it for the duration of the war, having already done so during World War I as the colonial system unraveled. So basically, the West sent the traumatized survivors of a genocide it had perpetrated to a region that it had alternately dominated and fought over, and established a new nation under its own authority with relatively little input from neighboring countries.

To this, add deep-seated religious conflict. Recall that Christians had been attempting to reconquer the Levant from Islamic rule for literally a thousand years beginning with the Crusades. Establishing a permanent nation of Israel smack dab in this disputed territory came across, not entirely inaccurately, as the West's way of cynically exploiting the genocide of a people to achieve a long-desired outcome. This energized the argument over what did and did not constitute the role of the West in the Islamic world. So the West did not leave the new government of Israel in a great position in the first place, and the cascading series of existential threats, violent crackdowns, and border disputes that have followed in the seven decades since were a direct result.

NATO AND THE WARSAW PACT

The Lowering of the Iron Curtain

"People are always shouting that they want to create a better future. It's not true. The future is an apathetic void of no interest to anyone....The only reason people want to be masters of the future is to change the past. They are fighting for access to the laboratories where photographs are retouched and biographies and histories rewritten."

—Milan Kundera (1929–), author

Would you be willing to destroy the world for an idea? For most of the second half of the twentieth century this wasn't an abstract question. The United States and the USSR (Union of Soviet Socialist Republics) jockeyed for regional influence, attempted to outshine each other in technological achievement, engaged in espionage on an unprecedented scale and with unprecedented sophistication, and each accumulated enough nuclear weapons to destroy the world many times over. The fact that humanity survived this period is something of an absurd miracle.

The goal, at least in theory, was abstract and economic: the United States represented free market capitalism, while the USSR represented Communism. But nothing is ever *just* about economics—not even economics itself. The concepts of Communism and capitalism became proxies for the real differences between the world powers: competing hierarchies of power and competing circles of trust.

Alexander Dubček

Beginning in January 1968, during a period known as the Prague Spring, Czechoslovakia operated under a rare combination of doctrines: Communism and respect for human rights. The newly appointed Czech general secretary, Alexander Dubček (1921–1992), referred to this new approach to politics as "socialism with a human face." Unfortunately for Dubček and the people of Czechoslovakia, the Soviet Union regarded this experiment as dangerous and ended it by invasion in August of the same year.

THE ORIGINS OF NATO

In 1948 the Soviet Union claimed control over Czechoslovakia. Europe soon became divided by an "iron curtain"—the symbolic boundary dividing Europe into two separate areas. And the division between capitalist western Germany and Communist eastern Germany would become represented, in 1961, by a literal wall between them to create two countries: West Germany and East Germany.

To strengthen the deterrent against Soviet control over the region, twelve nations—the United States, Britain, France, Belgium, Canada, Denmark, Iceland, Italy, Luxembourg, the Netherlands, Norway, and Portugal—signed a compact in 1949 called the North Atlantic Treaty. The signatories became members of what was to be known as the North Atlantic Treaty Organization (NATO). It has been in effect ever since, having grown to twenty-nine members in the intervening years. Article 5 of the pact compels that its members, in the event one of them is attacked, "will assist the Party or Parties so attacked." However, the only time Article 5 has ever been invoked was after the terrorist attacks of September 11, 2001, in the United States.

THE WARSAW PACT

In 1955 the USSR and seven other Communist nations signed the Warsaw Pact, a similar pledge of mutual defense, creating, in effect, a Communist counterpart to NATO. The original members were the Soviet Union, Albania, Bulgaria, Czechoslovakia, East Germany, Hungary, Poland, and Romania. The Warsaw Pact was dissolved in 1991 following the collapse of the Soviet Union.

First, Second, and Third World

During the Cold War, Western journalists divided the world into three categories:

- The First World, made up of countries affiliated or allied with NATO
- The Second World, made up of countries affiliated with or allied with the Warsaw Pact
- The Third World, made up of all other countries

Since Third World countries tended to be developing nations with high amounts of political volatility, the term *Third World* became something of a pejorative. But as it was originally conceived, it was anything but. The man who coined the term in 1952, the French historian Alfred Sauvy (1898–1990), compared the Third World to the Third Estate during the French Revolution— the part of society that, marginalized from power for generations, ultimately emerged victorious.

The primary purpose of the Warsaw Pact was to serve as a counterbalance to NATO. Like the North Atlantic Treaty, the Warsaw Pact included an Article 5 requiring all members to come to each other's aid in the event of attack. Fortunately for the world, the nightmare scenario of a head-on nuclear confrontation between NATO and the Warsaw Pact never materialized.

THE UNITED NATIONS AND HUMAN RIGHTS

Jus Gentium and Jus Civile

"There is no such thing as the State
And no one exists alone;
Hunger allows no choice
To the citizen or the police;
We must love one another or die."

—W.H. Auden (1907–1973), poet

In the aftermath of World War II, the people of the world woke from the threat of fascism and the unprecedented slaughter that came with it to find that they'd been given a second chance. Like the biblical Noah, the world had survived forty days and forty nights of rain and had to learn to walk on dry land again. But there was no rainbow to guarantee that the world would not be destroyed again, and the horrifying mechanical efficiency of the Holocaust and the equally horrifying apocalyptic threat posed by nuclear war raised very serious doubts about whether humanity itself would survive much longer. World War I, the first so-called "war to end all wars," had only presaged a second, more horrifying sequel. It seemed unlikely that humanity could survive a third installment.

It soon became clear that reform *within* nations would not be enough. But reform *among* nations—a standard that demanded peace and cooperation—could prevent the world from lapsing into fascism again, or at least prevent fascist nations from gathering the kind of unchecked power the Axis had accumulated. The global campaign for human rights and world peace wasn't entirely successful. But it was partially successful, and we may owe our lives to that partial success.

JUS GENTIUM

In ancient Roman law, which formed the philosophical basis for all Western law, law was essentially divided into two categories:

- *Jus civile* (Latin: "law of citizens")
- *Jus gentium* (Latin: "law of nations")

This distinction dates all the way back to Sumer, the first urban civilization. Legal documents describing purchases and imposing penalties constituted *jus civile* law applicable only in Sumer, while documents that appealed to a broader sense of justice affirmed the existence of some *jus gentium* standards that applied to everyone. The most notable of these was the "Praise Poem of Urukagina" (ca. 2350 B.C.E.), which appealed to universal standards of human rights and called on rulers to apply universal standards of law and social welfare so as to "never subjugate the waif and the widow to the powerful."

Later on in the Hebrew Bible, the Noachide commandments condemned murder, robbery, and cruelty to animals among all of humanity, not just the Jewish people (Genesis 9:5–6). And as we've discussed in previous chapters, both Cyrus the Great of the Persian

Empire and the Indian emperor Ashoka affirmed the existence of universal standards of human rights that were applicable under their domains. Many other subsequent rulers, in manners great and small, have done the same thing. In particular, Christianity and Islam—the two religious ideologies that have dominated the world for over a thousand years—both affirm universal standards of human rights, though it is not common for rulers in either tradition to consistently acknowledge them.

More recently, World War II brought about a global crisis of faith, of sorts. Faced with the Holocaust's unprecedentedly efficient large-scale slaughter and the new threat of nuclear annihilation, a committee—chaired by founding United Nations (UN) diplomat and widowed former US first lady Eleanor Roosevelt (1884–1962)—wrote the Universal Declaration of Human Rights, the first human rights agreement adopted by the UN. The next year, the international community adopted an extensive, revised version of the Geneva Conventions, a series of agreements on the treatment of soldiers and civilians during times of conflict.

The sections of the charter are as follows:

- Preamble: Defines and defends the concept of human rights.
- Article 1: Establishes that people have rights from birth, not citizenship.
- Article 2: Bans discrimination in a general sense.
- Article 3: Declares individual right to life, liberty, and security.
- Article 4: Bans slavery.
- Article 5: Bans torture.
- Article 6: Declares that rights should apply everywhere.
- Article 7: Requires equal protection without discrimination.
- Article 8: Requires nations to protect residents' human rights.

- Article 9: Bans arbitrary punishments.
- Article 10: Requires fair trials in criminal proceedings.
- Article 11: Requires presumption of innocence and access to legal counsel.
- Article 12: Bans harassment and defamation.
- Article 13: Protects freedom to travel.
- Article 14: Protects the right to legal asylum.
- Article 15: Protects the right to nationality.
- Article 16: Protects the right to marry and bans forced marriages.
- Article 17: Protects the right to property.
- Article 18: Protects freedom of religion.
- Article 19: Protects freedom of speech.
- Article 20: Protects freedom of assembly.
- Article 21: Protects voting rights.
- Article 22: Protects social security.
- Article 23: Protects freedom to work, equal pay, and trade unions.
- Article 24: Protects vacations and rest/leisure hours.
- Article 25: Protects social safety net, especially for mothers and children.
- Article 26: Protects the right to an education.
- Article 27: Protects intellectual rights, arts, and the sciences.
- Article 28: Calls for international structures to protect human rights.
- Article 29: Articulates a personal duty to protect the rights of others.

Since that time, the United Nations has adopted a series of nine more specific human rights treaties, each connected to a committee that reports on countries' compliance. These treaties are:

- The International Convention on the Elimination of All Forms of Racial Discrimination (1965)
- The International Covenant on Civil and Political Rights (1966)
- The International Covenant on Economic, Social and Cultural Rights (1966)
- The Convention on the Elimination of All Forms of Discrimination Against Women (1979)
- The Convention Against Torture and Other Cruel, Inhuman or Degrading Treatment or Punishment (1984)
- The Convention on the Rights of the Child (1989)
- The International Convention on the Protection of the Rights of All Migrant Workers and Members of Their Families (1990)
- The International Convention for the Protection of All Persons from Enforced Disappearance (2006)
- The Convention on the Rights of Persons with Disabilities (2006)

DEFINING GENOCIDE

While studying what we now call the Armenian Genocide (1915–1917) in Turkey, the Polish attorney Raphael Lemkin (1900–1959) coined the term *barbarity* to refer to large-scale atrocities. But he felt that the term was inadequate. After Lemkin, who was Jewish, lost forty-nine family members in the Holocaust, he recognized the need for a new moral vocabulary to describe this type of highly targeted large-scale racist violence. "We are in the presence," the British prime minister Winston Churchill remarked at the time, "of a crime without a name." Lemkin gave it a new name: *genocide*. He was the first to use the term, and the first to define it. As he wrote at the time in *Axis Rule in Occupied Europe* (1944):

"New conceptions require new terms. By 'genocide' we mean the destruction of a nation or of an ethnic group. This new word, coined by the author to denote an old practice in its modern development, is made from the ancient Greek word *genos* (race, tribe) and the Latin *cide* (killing), thus corresponding in its formation to such words as tyrannicide, homicide, infanticide, etc. Generally speaking, genocide does not necessarily mean the immediate destruction of a nation, except when accomplished by mass killings of all members of a nation. It is intended rather to signify a coordinated plan of different actions aiming at the destruction of essential foundations of the life of national groups, with the aim of annihilating the groups themselves."

Lemkin's framework has become the predominant lens through which we see these kinds of large-scale atrocities. In 1948 the UN General Assembly Resolution 260—better known as the Convention on the Prevention and Punishment of the Crime of Genocide—was drafted and passed based directly, in large part, on Lemkin's work.

There have also been attempts to create actual courts to try people for war crimes and other human rights violations. The most successful global human rights court has been the International Criminal Court (ICC), located in the Dutch city of The Hague. This court is the descendant of the International Military Tribunal that tried Nazi war criminals in 1945 and 1946, and it has indicted forty individuals since its founding in 1998. More specific circumstances often justify the creation of new human rights courts. The International Criminal Tribunal for the former Yugoslavia, established by the UN in 1993, indicted 161 former Bosnian war criminals—over four times the number of people ever indicted by the ICC.

PASSIVE RESISTANCE AND THE ACTIVIST TRADITION

Scholl, Gandhi, King

"We need, in every community, a group of angelic troublemakers. Our power is in our ability to make things unworkable. The only weapon we have is our bodies. And we need to tuck them in places so wheels don't turn."
—Bayard Rustin (1912–1987), American civil rights activist and organizer

---

The American political scientist Gene Sharp (1928–) has identified no fewer than 198 effective methods of nonviolent activism, ranging from skywriting to boycotts to general strikes to rude gestures. He didn't come up with this list on his own; rather, he studied the masters of twentieth-century activism and took notes. As we look ahead to an uncertain future and brainstorm opportunities to influence it, we could do worse.

Among the many activists who have inspired nonviolent passive resistance over the course of the twentieth century, three stand out. They were:

- Sophie Scholl (1921–1943), who organized anti-Nazi protestors at the University of Munich in an informal group called the White Rose Society. When she was caught distributing pamphlets condemning Nazi violence, she was summarily executed for treason.

- Mohandas Gandhi (1869–1948), Indian attorney, philosopher, and leader of the world's largest independence movement. Although he lived to see his country successfully achieve its independence from Great Britain, he was assassinated by an anti-Muslim Hindu nationalist who objected to Gandhi's willingness to build Hindu-Muslim alliances.
- Martin Luther King Jr. (1929–1968), an African-American civil rights organizer and second-generation Baptist minister who organized boycotts, marches, and other disruptive actions to break down the system of racial discrimination and segregation in the South. His work led directly, among other things, to the passage of the US Civil Rights Act of 1964. He was assassinated by white nationalist James Earl Ray, though many suspect (and a 1999 civil jury ruled) that Ray did not act alone.

Of course, justified violent resistance has certainly played an important role in the history of the twentieth century as well. During World War II, for example, without the French and Italian Resistance, Allied prospects in Nazi-occupied countries would have been far less promising. And one of the reasons for the success of nonviolent revolutionaries such as King and Gandhi—and one of the temporary guarantors of their safety—was the possibility that their more militant contemporaries might take over, and arm, their respective movements.

This is a challenge nonviolent protestors have always faced: to prove, by the effectiveness of their work, that they are not merely more respectable and less dangerous alternatives to violent protest, but rather that they represent a fundamentally better way to enact democratic reform. The degree to which they can accurately make this claim remains a subject of intense debate, and even the most committed practitioners of nonviolent resistance, such as Gandhi and King, have admitted that there are circumstances under which more violent methods are permissible.

Satyagraha

Gandhi called his philosophy of nonviolent passive resistance *satyagraha*, which loosely translates to "stubborn truth." The idea wasn't that it would be abstract or convenient for its targets; far from it. The idea is that it's possible to wear out an oppressive power structure by literally out-stubborning it.

TWILIGHT OF EMPIRES

The Age of Revolution

"When we revolt, it's not for a particular culture. We revolt simply because, for many reasons, we can no longer breathe."

—Frantz Fanon (1925–1961), author

Between the imperial scrambles of the early twentieth century and the Cold War of the mid- and latter-twentieth, the massive European empires and their ideologies had all had their say. But actual human beings trying to go about their daily lives *hadn't* necessarily had their say, and what was left of the European domination of the world would soon come to an end. By the end of the twentieth century, the countries of Europe ruled over the continent of Europe and very little else.

HOW TO LOSE AN EMPIRE IN TEN DECADES

It's hard to overstate just how powerful Europe and the European-founded United States were at the beginning of the twentieth century, but mathematics may give us a clue. In 1900 the great Austrian cartographer Alexander Supan (1847–1920) calculated the full extent of European dominance in percentages. Europe and the United States collectively controlled, at the time, 100 percent of

Europe (obviously), 100 percent of Australia, 98.9 percent of Polynesia, 90.4 percent of Africa, 56.5 percent of Asia, and 27.2 percent of the Americas. That means that in 1900, Europe and the United States collectively controlled 62.5 percent, excluding Antarctica, of the entire land mass of Earth.

By the end of the century, they'd lost almost all of it to various national independence movements. The British Empire, the largest empire in the history of the world, was particularly hard hit—going from controlling 13.7 million square miles in 1920 to controlling only part of the 122,000-square-mile British Isles less than a century later (with possible Northern Irish and Scottish independence referendums on the way). Other European empires lost their colonies too, and the relative importance of Europe in the world declined considerably. As industrialization and economic power have spread throughout Europe's former subject nations, it's safe to say the continent will never be that important again.

THE FORMER BRITISH EMPIRE	
Country	Year of Independence
New Zealand	1907
South Africa	1910
Egypt	1922
Ireland (except Northern Ireland)	1922
Canada	1931
Australia	1942
India	1947
Israel-Palestine	1948
Myanmar (Burma)	1948
Sri Lanka	1948
Pakistan	1956

Sudan	1956
Ghana	1957
Malaysia	1957
Cyprus	1960
Nigeria	1960
Cameroon	1961
Sierra Leone	1961
Tanzania	1961
Jamaica	1962
Trinidad and Tobago	1962
Uganda	1962
Kenya	1963
Malawi	1964
Malta	1964
Zambia	1964
Gambia	1965
Maldives	1965
Barbados	1966
Botswana	1966
Guyana	1966
Lesotho	1966
Yemen	1967
Mauritius	1968
Swaziland	1968
Fiji	1970
Tonga	1970
Bahrain	1971
Qatar	1971
United Arab Emirates	1971

The Bahamas	1973
Grenada	1974
Seychelles	1976
Dominica	1978
Solomon Islands	1978
Tuvalu	1978
Kiribati	1979
St. Lucia	1979
St. Vincent and the Grenadines	1979
Zimbabwe (formerly Rhodesia)	1980
Antigua and Barbuda	1981
Belize	1981
St. Kitts and Nevis	1983
Brunei	1984

You Say You Want a Revolution

The twentieth century was one in which many nations and colonies broke free from larger empires, but the story didn't begin with New Zealand in 1907, nor were those who rebelled against these empires prior to 1907 always doomed to failure. The British Empire had to contend with with its defeat at the hands of the colonial Americans led by George Washington (1732–1799). The French under Napoleon were soundly defeated by an army of slaves organized, and initially led, by the strategic genius Toussaint-Louverture (1743–1803), and the result has been more than two centuries of Haitian independence. And the Spanish army in Latin America snapped under the weight of an independence movement led by Simón Bolívar (1783–1830); Bolivia bears his name, but Colombia, Ecuador, Panama, Peru, and Venezuela also achieved independence under his movement's banner. For as long as there have been empires, there have been rebels. And sometimes—not often, but sometimes—the rebels win.

WOMEN'S LIBERATION IN THE AGE OF MASS MEDIA

The Second Wave

"If the shoe doesn't fit, must we change the foot?"

—Gloria Steinem (1934–)

In her bestseller *The Feminine Mystique* (1963), Betty Friedan, founding president of the National Organization for Women (NOW), wrote of "the problem that has no name": the oppressive rigidity of a life forcibly channeled into full-time marriage and full-time motherhood. Conventional wisdom says that women's liberation, also known as second-wave feminism, came about as a side effect of women recognizing that they could manage the civilian workforce during World War II—but it's unlikely that this came as much of a surprise to women as a group. Organizing to make workplace equality a reality, as a matter of law and cultural expectation, was another matter entirely.

First-wave feminism had already achieved its primary objective in most of the West: ending large-scale gender-based voting discrimination. This gave women a new tool to take on some of the other forms of gender-based discrimination that had been accepted as customary by politicians of the past. Of special interest to second-wave activists was the workforce. Gender-based discrimination was rampant, with women expected (and, in many instances, effectively forced) to live lives dedicated to full-time unpaid domestic work. Liberation from this expectation was at the center of the second-wave feminist movement. Other issues taken on by the second-wave movement included laws against sexual assault, access to birth control and abortion, and the right to own property. But nothing was more central to the second wave than eliminating the workplace discrimination that prevented women from achieving large-scale economic power on their own behalf.

Intersectionality

For as long as there has been a women's movement in the West, women of color have recognized that it hasn't done a great job of addressing issues that fall outside of the milieu of a middle-class white woman's life. In 1896, African-American feminist Mary Church Terrell (1863–1954) cocreated the National Association of Colored Women to point out intersections between the work of feminists and those of the early racial justice movement. But race and gender aren't the only intersections; the feminist movement tends to overlook disabled women, for example, while the disability rights movement tends to prioritize disabled men. Most potential targets of discrimination are attacked on multiple fronts—race, gender, sexual orientation, gender identity, disability status, class, national origin, age, and so on—whereas movements that combat a particular discrimination tend to fight on only one front at a time.

In 1989, Columbia legal scholar and perennial Supreme Court shortlister Kimberlé Crenshaw (1959–) invented the term "intersectionality" to refer to perspectives that, like Terrell's, acknowledge that people can be targeted by more than one form of oppression at a time. The term has since become a major part of the contemporary feminist vocabulary.

While the most egregious forms of workplace discrimination were technically prohibited by legislation such as the US Civil Rights Act of 1964 and the British Sex Discrimination Act 1975, a 2016 study by the World Economic Forum (WEF) found that, fifty years after the beginning of the second wave, a gender-based wage gap still exists in every country on Earth. Iceland, where a woman earns an average of eighty-eight cents per every dollar a man earns, outperforms every other nation on Earth in this regard; at the bottom of the list is Yemen, where the figure is a mere fifty-two cents. But nations celebrated for the progress they made during the second-wave movement, such as Britain (seventy-five cents) and the United States (seventy-two cents), don't even place in the top ten and are outperformed by many countries that are often stereotyped as less progressive on gender, such as Rwanda (eighty cents) and Nicaragua (seventy-eight cents).

KOREA, VIETNAM, AND AFGHANISTAN

The Cold War Goes Hot

"If we had focused on the balance of forces, we would have been defeated in
two hours. We were waging a people's war."

—Võ Nguyên Giáp (1911–2013), North Vietnamese minister of defense

---

One of the most grotesque things about the Cold War was the casual
attitude both the United States and the USSR had toward massive
third-party casualties. The USSR intentionally prodded and escalated
US involvement in Vietnam during the late 1960s and early 1970s
that would ultimately claim the lives of 1.5 million Vietnamese, and
the United States in turn intentionally prodded and escalated Soviet
involvement in Afghanistan during the 1980s that would ultimately
claim the lives of two million Afghans.

The nations that "won" both wars weren't the countries that actually fought them; they were the agent provocateurs who intentionally
escalated them for strategic reasons. History can't exactly record
that the USSR won the Vietnam War, and that the United States won
the Soviet-Afghan War, but these were the effective outcomes. They
were traps. And the vast majority of their victims were neither US
nor Soviet.

THE COST OF EMPIRE

Both NATO and the Warsaw Pact nations had access to enough nuclear weapons to destroy Earth many times over, so the prospect of a "hot war" of direct combat, after the fashion of World War II, just wasn't feasible. Or at least surviving such a war wouldn't have been feasible. So instead of nuking the planet, the United States and Soviet Union clashed in a series of wars that were relatively safe for their own civilians, but had a horrifying large-scale effect on the civilian populations of the countries they fought over.

The first major conflict of this kind was the Korean War (1950–1953), following the invasion of democratic South Korea by the Communist government of North Korea. China and the Soviet Union supported the North, the United States supported the South, and the war that resulted from all of this claimed the lives of 2.7 million Korean civilians. This war has never technically ended. Seven decades later, North and South Korea still operate as two separate countries in cease-fire, with a heavily mined demilitarized zone separating them.

The Soviets intervened less directly in the Vietnam War (1955–1975), where Communist North Vietnam—following the Korean model—invaded the nationalistic Republic of Vietnam to the south in an effort to unify the country by force. The United States came to the aid of South Vietnam, but never had a clearly articulated exit strategy or list of achievable objectives. After more than a decade of military involvement under three presidents with relatively little to show for it, the United States withdrew from the war and North Vietnam took control in 1976.

The Soviets found themselves in a similar situation in 1978, after the Communist People's Democratic Party of Afghanistan took control of Afghanistan and began a series of secular reforms. The

Soviets sent troops to protect the new government, the United States covertly assisted religious militias who sought to overthrow it, and the result was a decade of fighting that drained the Soviet military and later led, indirectly, to the rise of two terrorist organizations, the Taliban and al-Qaeda.

All three instances represented the same problem for the United States and the Soviet Union: each country had become such a vanguard for its respective ideology that *not* intervening in these sorts of cases would have been widely interpreted as a sign of military weakness. Just as had happened in the Crusades, two nations became so powerful that their leaders felt that they were not only entitled to carve up the world between them, but that they actually had an active responsibility to do so.

Mujahideen

Although the term *mujahideen* is now used in the West to refer to Islamic guerrilla fighters, it actually refers to anyone who is involved in jihad, whether they are doing charitable work (a jihad against human suffering and need), spreading the faith as missionaries (a jihad against despair), or teaching Islamic theology at a university (a jihad against ignorance).

THE NEOLIBERAL ORDER

Free Market Capitalism in the West

"When I ran for president seventeen years ago, I was told I was behind the times. Now everybody tells me I was ahead of my time. All I can say is that time certainly is an elusive companion."

—Barry Goldwater (1909–1998), from a 1981 speech

The European empires that colonized the West beginning in the sixteenth century were mercantile. They fed conquest, enslavement, and genocide through the same kinds of trade channels, and with the same kind of commercial philosophy, that they had used to trade fabric and spices. So it would be a mistake to say that the economic philosophy we call free market capitalism began as a conversation among political philosophers or economists. It began with haggling. That said, there was a moment on the evening of September 14, 1974, when economist Arthur Laffer, having dinner at the Two Continents Restaurant in Washington, DC, with Dick Cheney and Donald Rumsfeld, scribbled something on a napkin that would change global politics forever.

On the white cloth napkin, now on display at the National Museum of American History, is a simple curved line chart intended to show the relationship between taxation and government revenue. Tax 0 percent, and the government gets nothing. Tax 100 percent, Laffer argued, and the government still gets nothing—because people have no incentive to earn money they'll just give away in taxes anyway.

Somewhere between those numbers is a sweet spot: a tax rate low enough to incentivize earnings, but high enough to fund essential government programs. And while reaching that number can require us to raise taxes, it can far more often, Laffer argued, require us to cut them. This idea—called supply-side economics by its supporters, and trickle-down economics by its critics—has, to varying degrees, influenced fiscally conservative social policy ever since, in every major party, and on every continent.

NEOLIBERALISM AND NEOCONSERVATISM

No prominent elected officials regularly call themselves neoliberals or neoconservatives, and it's rare to find two thinkers who agree on exactly what the terms mean. But the terms do have widely accepted general meanings in academic circles, however much they may blur at the edges.

To begin with it's important to note that "liberal" and "conservative" are not antonyms in this context and are, in fact, used to refer to some of the same general trends. What an economist calls "liberal" is free market capitalism—minimal taxation and minimal financial regulation—which is the exact opposite of what we call liberal in politics. So if an economist calls you a liberal and a politician calls you a conservative, they're actually saying the same thing.

In economics, neoliberalism refers to the liberal backlash against the expansion of social welfare programs, and specifically to the post-1970, antiwelfare strain of capitalism usually advocated by people who believe in supply-side economics in some form. It does not refer to all forms of capitalism, though neoliberal politics are reflected in both major US political parties.

In left-wing political parties, neoliberal policies are usually offered up as a compromise rather than an across-the-board pledge. US President Bill Clinton's 1992 campaign promise to "end welfare as we know it" and transition to a "welfare-to-work" system is a clear example of a neoliberal policy, despite the fact that Clinton protected and even expanded some unrelated social welfare programs.

Keynesian Economics versus Austerity

When a country is in a recession, should its government spend *more* money or *less*? On a surface level, there are good arguments for each.

The best argument for spending *more* money to get out of a bad economic situation was the 1930s Great Depression in the United States, where massively increased federal spending under President Franklin D. Roosevelt (1882–1945) appeared to steer the economy aright by loaning public-sector money into the private sector to create jobs and promote social welfare. This is traditionally the approach favored by the British economist John Maynard Keynes (1883–1946), whose overall system, referred to as Keynesian economics, is the most widely accepted economic philosophy in Western academic circles.

Neoliberalism favors an alternate approach called *austerity*. Inspired by supply-side economics, austerity operates on the belief that if you cut taxes, especially for investors and corporations, it will increase private-sector spending and investment, precluding the need for dramatic government intervention. Of course, in order to cut taxes you need to *decrease* government spending. This creates an unpopular situation where a large number of people, already driven into poverty during a recession, find that their government support system is also shrinking.

Austerity hasn't produced a clear success story yet. History has shown so far that investors tend to hold on to their money during recessions, which are also not generally regarded as ideal times for private corporations to dramatically expand their workforce. But neoliberals continue to experiment with different austerity policies, looking for a private-sector, supply-side solution to recessions that can rescue an economy without increasing taxes or the size of the government.

Neoconservatism in domestic policy refers essentially to the same rejection of social welfare policy that we see in neoliberalism, along with the same implicit embrace of supply-side economics. But the word *neoconservatism* is more commonly used today to refer to a foreign policy agenda that emphasizes the aggressive expansion of Western-style government. During the Cold War, neoconservatives targeted nations that flirted with Communist ideology. But after the collapse of the Soviet Union—and especially after the September 11 attacks—the focus shifted to "rogue nations": states that are defined as badly behaved, either because they had violated Western demands in their acquisition of weapons of mass destruction or because they're state sponsors of terrorism. Like neoliberalism, neoconservative foreign policy is found in both conservative and liberal political parties. For example, in the aftermath of September 11, US President George Bush (of the right-wing GOP) and British Prime Minister Tony Blair (of the left-wing Labour Party) became the most visible advocates of neoconservative foreign policies.

THE PARADOX OF IRANIAN DEMOCRACY

The Shah and the Ayatollah

"The revolution is like a bicycle. When the wheels don't turn, it falls."
—Marjane Satrapi (1969–), author of
Persepolis: The Story of a Childhood (2000)

One of the tragic consequences of the Cold War is that both the United States and the USSR fought over the right to dominate countries whose people didn't want to be dominated in the first place. No region of the world was more deeply harmed by this ridiculous dynamic than the Middle East, and Iran is an especially poignant case in point.

In April 1951 the people of Iran had largely united behind their new secular democratic prime minister, Mohammad Mossadegh (1882–1967). He had been elected to that office by the Iranian parliament with the blessing of the reigning shah, Mohammad Reza Pahlavi (1919–1980). Mossadegh promised to restore control over Iranian resources to the people, including Iran's oil, which had been under the control of BP (formerly British Petroleum) for four decades. Unfortunately for Iran, the United States feared that nationalizing the country's oil revenue would nudge the country too much in the direction of Communism—and, in any case, did not want to see BP lose profits. In August 1953 the CIA supported the coup that deposed

Mossadegh and installed an unpopular military dictatorship in his place. This set the stage for one of the most tragic, and lasting, theocratic revolts of the past century.

In January 1979 the exiled Ayatollah Ruhollah Khomeini (1902–1989), a former legislator and longtime enemy of the shah, returned to Iran amidst cheers after the shah had fled. The secular democratic government that the revolutionaries hoped he would help lead was not to his liking. "I shall kick their teeth in," he said at the time. "I appoint the government." Khomeini got his wish, becoming Iran's first supreme leader. While Iran technically has an elected president and an elected legislature, the supreme leader has largely functioned with power comparable to that of a shah ever since.

THE STRUCTURE OF IRAN'S GOVERNMENT

The post-1979 Iranian federal government is essentially made up of five branches:

- **The supreme leader.** We tend to refer to supreme leaders as the Ayatollah (Arabic: "message from God"), but this is a convenience. Ayatollah is not a political title but is actually a religious honorific within Shiite Islam. In other words, there are many ayatollahs throughout the world, but there can be only one Iranian supreme leader at a given time (and it would be constitutionally permissible, albeit unprecedented, to select a layperson for the position). Although he functionally has the power of a dictator, the supreme leader serves at the pleasure of the Assembly of Experts, who theoretically have the power to impeach him at any time. There have been only two supreme leaders since 1979: Supreme Leader Ayatollah Ruhollah Khomeini, who served from 1979 to 1989, and Supreme Leader Ayatollah Ali Khamenei (1939–), who has served since 1989.

- **The president.** Elected by the people to a four-year term (and term limited at eight years), the president of Iran has variable amounts of executive power delegated to him by the supreme leader. While the president himself can't contradict the supreme leader, the election of one president or another can tell the supreme leader the direction Iranian voters want the country to go. There have been seven presidents, the four most influential being the future Supreme Leader Ali Khamenei (who served from 1981 to 1989), the notoriously bellicose and conservative Mahmoud Ahmadinejad (who served from 2005 to 2013), and the reformers Mohammad Khatami (who served from 1997 to 2005) and Hassan Rouhani (who has served since 2013).

- **The Guardian Council.** Made up of twelve senior clerics—six appointed by the supreme leader, six by parliament—this is essentially a combination judicial and religious court whose duty is to ensure that government policies are consistent with both the national constitution and Shiite theology as they interpret it.

- **The Assembly of Experts.** A group of eighty-eight ayatollahs who are required to meet every six months to assess the supreme leader's fitness for duty and, when necessary, to meet in a special session to replace the supreme leader. Candidates for the Assembly are elected by voters but must first be approved by the Guardian Council.

- **The Iranian parliament, officially known as the Islamic Consultative Assembly.** Made up of 290 members (both men and women) who are elected directly by the people and serve a standard legislative role: proposing and passing legislation, making budgetary decisions, and so forth. While this branch of government does not enjoy the level of independence from the supreme leader that most elected parliaments have, its influence isn't purely symbolic, either.

Shirin Ebadi

Prior to the Revolution of 1979, Iranian culture had long been progressive on gender issues. When the new fundamentalist regime took power, however, many young women who had become judges were effectively fired on the spot. Among these was Shirin Ebadi (1947–), who would soon use her legal training to become an advocate for the rights of women and dissidents. In 2003, she received a Nobel Peace Prize for her work. After her family was threatened, and her husband beaten and detained, it became impossible for her to continue her work. She currently lives in exile in London.

THE DECLINE AND FALL OF THE SOVIET UNION

Lenin's Mausoleum

"I'm old and tired. Let them cope by themselves. I've done the main thing. Could anyone have dreamed of telling Stalin that he didn't suit us anymore and suggesting he retire? Not even a wet spot would have remained where we had been standing. Now everything is different. The fear is gone, and we can talk as equals. That's my contribution. I won't put up a fight."
—Nikita Khrushchev (1894–1971), following his removal as general secretary

Toward the end of the eighteenth century, two writers debated the relative merits of the French Revolution and, implicitly, the moral implications of the colonists' revolution against the British government in North America. The more conservative of the two men, the Irish parliamentarian Edmund Burke (1729–1797), argued that incrementalism was generally preferable to revolution—that the most humane thing you can do when you're reforming something is preserve as many institutions as possible, and proceed with caution so that any necessary changes involve as little trauma as possible. The more radical English-American pamphleteer Thomas Paine (1737–1809) disagreed strongly with Burke, arguing that the real problems of the world are deeply seated enough that only violent, unpleasant, institution-shattering revolution can fix them.

The Union of Soviet Socialist Republics (USSR) was, to a greater degree than even the United States, a case study in Paine's approach. It was so radically different in philosophy from any government that had preceded it that the fact that it held together as long as it did, and with the level of commitment to its original principles that it did, is a testament to the power of political ideas. Although Paine is generally credited with having won the argument with Burke, the USSR serves as a cautionary reminder that powerful political ideas aren't enough.

REFORM AND COLLAPSE

The story of the twentieth century is, to a great extent, the story of civilizations created based on ideas that fell short of their goals because of personality cults. The Soviet Union had to struggle with this problem early with Vladimir Lenin, but Lenin, at least, was committed to some consistent version of Marxist ideology. The leader who would ultimately transform the Soviet Union into something more autocratic, and less grounded in traditional Communist goals, was also the leader who made it one of the most powerful nations on Earth: the brilliant but bloody-minded autocrat Joseph Stalin.

When Nikita Khrushchev (1894–1971) inherited the Soviet Union three years after Stalin's death, he made it his business to condemn the Stalinist personality cult and the worst of his atrocities. This would ultimately prove to be his undoing, as Communist hardliners loyal to Stalin's memory—and who still controlled most of the Soviet Communist Party—ousted Khrushchev from power after less than a decade and installed the more compliant Leonid Brezhnev (1906–1982). Brezhnev was no Stalin, but on his own scale he was brutal, oppressive, and intolerant of dissidents. His decision to crush the democratic reforms of the popular Czechoslovakian leader Alexander Dubček in 1968, putting an end to a cultural renaissance that he called "socialism with a human face" and historians would later call the Prague Spring, made it clear that the Soviet Union would not tolerate any innovations in Communist policy.

By the time the energetic young agriculturalist Mikhail Gorbachev (1931–) inherited leadership over the Soviet Union in 1985, the cost of this stagnation had become apparent. Gorbachev instituted a series of democratic reforms, and even promised elections, before Communist hardliners of the same ideological strain as those who had removed Khrushchev decided that enough was enough. But in removing Gorbachev from power in a military coup in July 1991, the Party leadership had a reckoning. They had dramatically underestimated the popularity of his reforms.

Glasnost and Perestroika

After the young and progressive Mikhail Gorbachev took the office of general secretary of the Communist Party in March 1985, relations between the East and the West began to warm up a little. Two buzzwords, *glasnost* and *perestroika*, were associated with Gorbachev's reforms.

The word *glasnost* (which can be loosely translated as "public voice") was originally popularized by founding Communist revolutionary Vladimir Lenin (1870–1924). It referred to the openness and transparency that he expected the new Soviet administration to represent. The secrecy, paranoia, and oppression of the Stalin era effectively destroyed mainstream use of the term. Until Gorbachev resurrected it, only dissident writers like Aleksandr Solzhenitsyn talked about glasnost.

The term *perestroika* ("spreading order") had a much more recent vintage. Popularized by Gorbachev's predecessor, General Secretary Yuri Andropov

(1914–1984), the term referred to reform efforts that even Soviet hardliners had recognized would become necessary in order to eliminate inefficient and exploitative bureaucracies.

In addition to glasnost and perestroika, Gorbachev less famously but no less urgently called for *uskoreniye* (economic growth), *khozrachyot* (profit), and *demokratizatsiya* (incremental democracy) as new strategies that he hoped would "activate the human factor" among his country's people. The question of what would have happened if he had been allowed to succeed in these reforms is one that historians have debated since the collapse of the Soviet Union, and will probably continue to debate for centuries to come.

The Soviet Union collapsed, and a rising new democratic Russia appeared primed to replace it. While Russia's trajectory toward democracy has been interrupted by the multidecade rule of autocrat Vladimir Putin (1952–), even his autocracy has technically featured regular multiparty elections—not free and fair elections of the type Gorbachev proposed, but elections just the same. The monstrous ambitions of Stalin and the asphyxiating stagnation of the Brezhnev era have become increasingly distant memories.

SOUTH AFRICA AND THE LEGACY OF APARTHEID

The Long Walk to Freedom

"In time, we shall be in a position to bestow on
South Africa the greatest possible gift: a more human face."
—Stephen Biko, martyred activist (1946–1977), from *I Write What I Like* (1978)

The bones would tell the story, in the end. In May 1997, when racial apartheid had finally been abolished and South Africa was governed by democratically elected leaders, the Truth and Reconciliation Commission dug up the long-undiscovered remains of Ntombikayise Priscilla Khubeka (1946–1987), an organizer who had died a decade earlier in the custody of South Africa's white supremacist police force.

According to the officers, who pled for amnesty, Khubeka's death had been an accident. They'd taken her into custody because of her suspected involvement in organizing political protests and, as was the custom of the day regarding black protestors, tortured her in search of information. They said she died during interrogation. But the Truth and Reconciliation Commission found something that conflicted with their story: a bullet hole in Khubeka's skull. We'll never know exactly why they murdered her; had she outsmarted or humiliated them in some way? Whatever their motive, the officers, who had never intended for the Commission to actually find Khubeka's body, hadn't told the truth. Their petition for amnesty was denied.

SEGREGATION AT ALL COSTS

One of the practical inconveniences that comes with invading another country to exploit its labor and resources is that the original residents of that country tend to outnumber the invaders. Britain discovered this the hard way at the Battle of Isandlwana, in January 1879, when the 1,200 heavily armed men of the 1st Battalion, 24th Foot were slaughtered by a larger and better-trained regiment of Zulu warriors armed with spears and shields. For the next several decades after that, three different groups attempted to establish control of the country:

- The original indigenous inhabitants, such as the Zulu and Xhosa, who had lived there for tens of thousands of years
- Dutch farmers, known as Boers, who had lived there for a little over a century
- British colonists, who had invaded less than a century earlier to keep the French out

Since Europe was out to conquer the world at the time, leaving the native South Africans alone wasn't an option. The British and the Boers fought over the territory during the First (1880–1881) and Second (1899–1902) Boer Wars. The British won a gentleman's victory and promised to will the country over to the Boers later. The Boer-led Republic of South Africa, founded in 1931, ultimately resulted from this long and messy process.

But the Boers faced a new problem: they wanted a white-run country, and 80 percent of the people who lived in their territory weren't white. Things came to a head during the 1948 election, when the centrist party led by veterans of the Boer War suggested racial integration and greater civil rights for black South Africans while a new, far-right party advocated taking radical steps in the opposite direction to segregate black South Africans from whites. The Boers chose to take the latter option. The result was a system of government called *apartheid* (Dutch Afrikaans for "held apart"). The new system of apartheid gave whites unchallenged authority over the operation of the South African government and exploitation of its resources, and criminalized racial integration.

We'll never know for certain exactly how many black activists the South African government killed during this period, but even the most conservative estimates range in the thousands. South African police were typically secretive—killing their targets one by one, hiding the bodies, and then denying involvement. But sometimes they took their violence public, as in the case of the 1960 Sharpeville massacre, where police fired into a crowd of thousands of protestors, killing sixty-nine and injuring hundreds. When the nation's black population protested, the government responded by detaining eighteen thousand activists and banning all major black-led political organizations, forcing the resistance underground. The most high-profile target of the raids was the prominent Xhosa activist Nelson Mandela (1918–2013), who was sentenced to life in prison in 1962.

But the South African government's efforts, however desperate, proved unsustainable as a long-term strategy. By 1990 the Republic of South Africa—worn out by decades of resistance and condemned by most of the world for its human rights abuses—could no longer sustainably carry the burden of apartheid. The incumbent president at the time, the recently elected F.W. de Klerk (1936–), ordered Mandela's release, legalized the long-banned national liberation movement African National Congress (ANC), and took initial steps toward reform. In a 1992 referendum a majority of white South African voters chose to abolish apartheid. The country's first multiracial elections followed in 1994, electing Mandela—now remembered as the father of modern South Africa—as its first black president. F.W. de Klerk, who along with Mandela had received a Nobel Peace Prize in 1993 for his efforts to end apartheid, served as his deputy.

The Truth and Reconciliation Commission

In criminal prosecutions, accomplices are often offered immunity in exchange for their testimony. The new postapartheid South African government attempted this by establishing the Truth and Reconciliation Commission (TRC) in July 1995. The TRC investigated more than seven thousand cases of politically motivated human rights abuses that had taken place between 1960 and 1994, granting amnesty in fewer than nine hundred cases. If the offender(s) withdrew the plea or were found to have lied about substantial elements of the offense, amnesty was not granted. Although relatively few prosecutions resulted from the TRC's work, it proved effective in uncovering details regarding the most notorious incidents. The TRC has served as a model for similar commissions in other countries with a history of human rights abuses.

SECTARIAN CONFLICT IN THE POST–COLD WAR WORLD

The Road from Damascus

"Fundamentalists look back to a 'golden age' before the irruption of modernity for inspiration, but they are not atavistically returning to the Middle Ages. All are intrinsically modern movements and could have appeared at no time other than our own. All are innovative and often radical in their reinterpretation of religion. As such, fundamentalism is an essential part of the modern scene."

—Karen Armstrong (1944–), from *Islam: A Short History* (2000)

On September 11, 2001, nineteen hijackers affiliated with the terrorist organization al-Qaeda hijacked four planes and crashed them into the World Trade Center in New York City, the Pentagon in Washington, DC, and an empty field in Pennsylvania. They killed an estimated 2,996 people in what was, by far, the single deadliest terrorist attack in modern history. The motive was unambiguously grounded in a bizarre interpretation of the Qur'an, popular among certain militant fundamentalist sects. In addition to prompting a series of wars and smaller-scale confrontations, it prompted an informal new Cold War, of sorts, based on mutual suspicion between those who felt they alone adhered to the values of the Christian West and those who felt that they alone upheld the values of the Islamic Middle East. Both groups had in common the need to express hostility toward the religiously and geographically diverse networks upon which the global economy depends.

The truth is that most large-scale ideologies have been weaponized to some degree or another. But there's something especially dangerous about the potential implications of a global religious conflict against which war, poverty, and even the promise of one's own death often prove to be inadequate deterrents.

TERROR AND COUNTERTERROR

Even prior to the twenty-first century, there were countless smaller-scale religiously motivated acts of terrorism. These include:

- The St. Nedelya Church massacre of Holy Thursday, April 1925, where militant antireligious members of the Bulgarian Communist Party bombed a church during a funeral, killing 150.
- The Air India Flight 182 hijacking of June 1985, where members of a neo-Sikh fundamentalist sect set off a bomb on a civilian aircraft over Ireland, killing 329.
- The Oklahoma City bombing of April 1995, where Timothy McVeigh, an associate of the white nationalist Christian Identity movement, bombed a US federal building, killing 168.
- The Aum Shinrikyo attack of July 1995, where followers of a neo-Buddhist doomsday prophet sprayed sarin gas in the Tokyo subway system, killing twelve and injuring more than 5,000.
- The Walisongo school massacre of May 2000, when Christian fundamentalists killed 191 targets (primarily Muslim children) in a central Indonesian port city.

No religious tradition, and no part of the world, is completely immune to violent sectarian conflict. The big three Western monotheisms—Judaism,

Christianity, and Islam—have well-documented violent histories to contend with, but Western readers who look for consistently peaceful traditions elsewhere are unlikely to find them. Genocidal Buddhist monks hunt down peaceful Rohingya Muslim families in Sri Lanka, violent Hindu nationalists routinely maim or execute women and girls in rural India, and as Stalin's legacy demonstrates, even those who reject religion entirely can end up slaughtering millions on ideological grounds. Those who identify other ideologies as intrinsically violent tend to use this as an excuse to target people who belong to those ideologies, continuing the cycle of violence.

Osama bin Laden

As a member of the CIA-backed mujahideen who fought the USSR in Afghanistan during the 1980s, Osama bin Laden (1957–2011) quickly distinguished himself as an effective military leader. But he also soon developed a reputation for exceptional cruelty, shocking the Middle Eastern press when he and his men raped, tortured, and killed as many as seven hundred Shiite civilians in northern Pakistan over a nine-day period in May 1988. Public response to the incident, later referred to as the Gilgit massacre, made bin Laden a pariah among Sunni militants and ultimately contributed to his decision to create a new organization: al-Qaeda.

After the Saudi royal family refused to accept al-Qaeda's help during the US-Allied Operation Desert Storm, choosing to accept US assistance instead, bin Laden turned against his former US patrons and became a sworn enemy of the West. Over the course of the 1990s the charismatic bin Laden found a second career as a populist demagogue, railing against the growing secularism he saw around him and condemning what he saw as the evils of Israel and the West. Many devout Sunnis in Saudi Arabia, Afghanistan, and Pakistan, who had their own reservations about the state of the world, initially felt that bin Laden's concerns mirrored their own.

During the same period, bin Laden also organized a series of terrorist attacks throughout the region. He found refuge in Pakistan, but it was only after the Taliban took control of Afghanistan in 1997 that bin Laden found a nation whose leaders had any serious interest in helping him turn his ideology into law.

Following the September 11 attacks and the US-Afghan War, bin Laden went into hiding. The man whose portrait had once decorated countless homes in the Middle East during the height of his popularity had become an invisible recluse who could only watch as thousands of militants he had personally recruited to the cause were killed during a series of counterterrorism campaigns. By the time bin Laden himself fell prey to US Navy SEALs in May 2011, al-Qaeda had functionally been destroyed and bin Laden himself had become more a symbol of cowardice than bravery. But his slow, bloody journey from US ally to bitter enemy illustrates, as well as any one person's life can, that the enemy of your enemy is not necessarily your friend.

The War on Terror (2001–present), initiated by the United States and Britain after the September 11 attacks, demonstrates this tendency in an especially striking way. Because of a series of notorious terrorist attacks over the past several decades perpetrated by Middle Eastern terrorist groups that identify themselves with Islam, Western leaders were able to press the idea that majority-Muslim nations needed to be reformed by the sword—an eerie reverberation of the logic behind the Crusades. The subsequent wars in Afghanistan (2001–2014) and Iraq (2003–2011) have collectively claimed the lives of more than 200,000 civilians, based on the most conservative credible estimates—more than sixty-five times as many civilians as were killed in the September 11 attacks themselves. Emerging regional terrorist groups have, in turn, cited these casualties as a rationale for years of horrific attacks that they have perpetrated against other innocent civilians, and so on. As the Nigerian proverb puts it: "When two elephants fight, it is the grass that suffers."

THE TWILIGHT OF WESTERN SUPREMACY

Nationalism and the Emerging Global Order

"Nationalism is like cheap alcohol: First it makes you drunk,
then it makes you blind, and then it kills you."
—Daniel Fried (1952–), former assistant US secretary of state

---

In his address before the International Peace Congress of 1849, the great French novelist Victor Hugo (1802–1885) spoke of the Europe that he hoped would one day rise. "A day will come," he said, "when the bullets and bombs are replaced by votes, by universal suffrage, by the venerable arbitration of a great supreme senate which will be to Europe what Parliament is to England, the Diet to Germany, and the Legislative Assembly to France."

His dream seemed to finally be within reach in 1993, when the 1991 Maastricht Treaty took effect and the European Union (EU) was officially formed. Based on common administrative instruments, human rights agreements, and an ambitious new continent-wide currency called the euro, the EU stood to become the most politically and geographically ambitious confederacy of member nations since the USSR. But old anxieties over shifting European demographics, coupled with interference from Russian president Vladimir Putin (1952–), have threatened to destroy the EU. And even if it survives, it has become increasingly clear that the West's status as the center of global economic power is rapidly drawing to a close.

ECONOMY AND ETHNICITY

For most of the past five hundred years, Europe has been the global center of economic and military power. It colonized most of the world and left the rest in fear. Even the United States and Russia, the two global powers that came to dominate the world during the past century, are functionally extensions of European power—Russia straddling the Eurasian border, and the United States as a former European colony. But as the rest of the world develops, Europe's economic and military advantages will diminish.

By 2050, experts believe the world's two largest economies will be those of China and India. The Global South—Latin America and sub-Saharan Africa—will be economically formidable players on the world stage. Islam will very likely have eclipsed Christianity as the world's largest religion, and the idea of a "superpower," a single nation that dominates the world, will have long since become ludicrous.

Meanwhile, as native birthrates decline and immigration continues, the United States and Europe are likely to become minority-white by 2050. For many white Americans and Europeans, this amounts to a two-pronged change in their identity: they're witnessing a decline in their countries' relative power at the same time they're witnessing a demographic shift in their own countries away from white majorities and toward more multiracial national identities.

In reaction to these long-term trends, white nationalist movements that promise to make their home countries "great" again by re-establishing their place in the world, while simultaneously preserving their majority-white demographics, have become more popular. Whether one is talking about the Donald Trump movement in the United States or the Geert Wilders movement in the Netherlands, Marine Le Pen's National Front in France, or Frauke Petry's

Alternative for Germany, critics of "globalism" and supporters of ethnic nationalism have achieved considerable influence in recent years.

One of their primary targets has been the European Union (EU) itself, as the EU—with its globalist mandate, human rights instruments, and willingness to ultimately accept the membership of majority-nonwhite European nations such as Turkey—runs counter to the interests of nationalism in general, and white nationalism in particular. The June 2016 Brexit referendum, in which a slim majority of UK voters elected to leave the EU as a reassertion of traditional British identity, was profoundly affected by fears of Turkish inclusion and large-scale nonwhite immigration. Wilders, Le Pen, and Petry are all similarly hostile to the EU, and wish to withdraw their respective countries from it.

Although economic and demographic realities would appear to doom the antiglobalist mission from the start, the movement appears to be growing rather than shrinking. It has already profoundly disrupted the global economy by way of Trump's election and the passage of Brexit, and its capacity to disrupt economic and military coalitions in the future is enormous.

WHY RACISM KEEPS COMING BACK

The growth of the international white nationalist movement in recent decades raises some unsettling questions about how exactly racism works. Historically, social sciences have taught that racism is something that's passed on from one generation to the next—but in the case of the Le Pen movement in France, and the online neo-Nazi movement in the United States, most of the bad actors seem to be young people whose parents and grandparents often have more progressive views on race than they do. So if racist sentiment isn't inherited, what causes it to spike? And what can be done about it?

There is some limited evidence to suggest that the *less* racist whites seem to be, the *more* likely they are to allow themselves to develop racist attitudes. One 2009 Stanford study, published in the *Journal of Experimental Social Psychology*, found that whites were significantly more likely to claim racist beliefs if first given an opportunity to say that they had voted for Barack Obama in the 2008 presidential election. Unrelated studies on the effect of moral self-licensing all seem to suggest a deeply cynical possibility: the less racist people *think* white people are, the more comfortable they are with revealing racist attitudes and behavior.

This would explain Le Pen's relative popularity among white French youth. Because they are assumed not to be racist, given their age, young French voters may feel more comfortable identifying with racist beliefs than older voters. This also helps to explain why civil rights movements are generally followed by a backlash period. For example, a white person who marched with Martin Luther King Jr. in 1964 and then voted for a segregationist like George Wallace for president in 1968 comes off as a complex, not single-mindedly racist, individual. As the Stanford study suggests, such individuals might be more likely to do the latter than they would be if they hadn't marched with Dr. King.

One characteristic often studied by political scientists and sociologists, white racial resentment, even reflects a widespread belief among whites that people of color owe them for past antiracist behavior. This sense of entitlement is itself a racist attitude, and can feed into future racist behavior.

As Western demographics continue to shift over the next few decades, the white nationalist movement may continue to grow in popularity among whites, even as whites gradually make up a smaller percentage of the population. This may ultimately lead to political dynamics even stranger than the ones we're living through right now.

Enoch Powell's Rivers of Blood

It's difficult to identify *exactly* when the mainstreaming of the European white nationalist movement began, but you could pick a less accurate date than April 20, 1968, the day the English lawmaker Enoch Powell (1912–1998) delivered his "rivers of blood" speech to a local conservative association. In the speech (so named because he quoted the Roman poet Virgil's premonition about "the River Tiber foaming with much blood"), Powell decried what he called the "avoidable evils" of ethnic diversity and multiculturalism, which he characterized as existential threats to Britain's white majority.

The white nationalist National Front had been founded a year earlier, but Powell—an avuncular, scholarly figure with a distinguished military record and decades of public service already behind him—was a giant of the mainstream British conservative movement, and his endorsement of these ideas had a far more virulent effect.

While the speech took Powell *out* of the mainstream (costing him his high-ranking leadership position within the Conservative Party), it had such a profound influence on right-wing politics in Britain and throughout Western Europe, that many observers credited it in part for Brexit, the early twenty-first century decision by Britain to withdraw from the European Union. In contrast to conservatives of Powell's time, who by and large condemned the speech and wanted nothing to do with it, Nigel Farage, who led the Brexit campaign, remarked in a 2014 newspaper interview that he felt "the basic principle [of the speech] is right."

THE FUTURE OF HISTORY

Humanity's Prognosis

"Art is the symbol of the two noblest human efforts:
to construct and refrain from destruction."
—Simone Weil (1909–1943), writer

In 1992, Stanford political scientist Francis Fukuyama's *The End of History and the Last Man* postulated that the world was on the verge of achieving liberal democracy, globalism, and the end of ethnic and sectarian strife—a coming era of peace so complete and profound that it would end human history as we know it. Now it's a quarter-century later, and the book hasn't aged so well. Liberal democracy is being tested in new ways, globalism has been sorely tested by recessions and various forms of populist nationalism, and ethnic and sectarian strife are doing just fine.

But that's what history is. There's a reason Fukuyama identified the end of history with the end of conflict. Once everything is peaceful and civilized, once we're all moving forward as a species, the traditional work of historians will be over. Nineteenth-century British writers quoted what they called a Chinese curse: "May you live in interesting times." We are living in interesting times. And when those interesting times end—when we rise completely over our squabbles, or are crushed completely beneath them—the work of history, as we have come to know it, will be done.

TOMORROW NEVER KNOWS

Writing of the French Revolution in *A Tale of Two Cities*, English novelist Charles Dickens (1812–1870) began his story with something that has become a cliché: "It was the best of times, it was the worst of times." Time, in general, tends to be like that. Case in point: the future is full of joy and promise, and it'll also kill us.

Reasons for Concern

The next few generations of humanity will need to deal with some existential threats that we haven't had to, and some of them are our fault. We'll either solve them and move on or not solve them and not move on. Examples include:

Global Climate Change

We've been dramatically transforming Earth's atmosphere over the past thousand years or so, and especially since the Industrial Revolution. This has already made Earth uninhabitable for as many as 140,000 species per year. If we don't enact dramatically unpopular policies to combat this effect, our species may join them.

But even if we don't make the world unsuitable for all of humanity, global climate change can contribute to national disasters, weaken agriculture, and flood out habitable land. Even if we as a species survive, many of us—especially those of us in poorer regions of the world—will not.

Disease

The world is more populous and urbanized than it has ever been, which means that we provide a larger breeding ground for infectious disease than there has ever been. The fact that a global pandemic has not recently wiped out a double-digit percentage of our species is lucky bordering on miraculous, and there's no guarantee that the pattern will hold.

Proliferation of Weapons of Mass Destruction

Access to chemical, nuclear, and biological weapons doesn't decrease from year to year. While the United States remains the only country to have used nuclear weapons in war, and it's been more than seventy years since that happened, it's much easier to invent weapons than it is to contain them.

Reasons for Hope

There are also advantages the next few generations of humanity will have that none of our predecessors had. Examples include:

Medicine

Today, medical science can give us artificial organs, in vitro fertilization, and full-body diagnostic scans; soon it will be able to give us customized organs, artificial wombs, and entire prosthetic bodies. Making these kinds of options accessible to everybody is a different matter entirely, of course, but in a relative sense we've gotten very good at keeping each other alive.

Information Technology and Social Media

The human world has a nervous system now, and while it doesn't connect everybody, it's getting close. Mobile smartphones in developing countries, in particular, are becoming cheaper and more ubiquitous. Facebook currently has two billion active users, representing over a quarter of the world's population, and the number of overall Internet users is significantly higher. Why is this relevant? Because two of the most significant problems we've faced as a species, histori-cally, have been our inability to communicate with each other in a timely manner and our inability to access information. We're closing in on both problems.

The New Agriculture

Genetically modified organisms (GMOs) are controversial, but they've already saved as many as a billion lives. Autonomous tractors, already a reality, will soon become cheap enough to make automated agricultural labor scalable. Lab-grown meat may cut down dramatically on the amount of land and resources currently necessary for livestock production. And these are among the *first* effects that new technologies are likely to have on our ability to grow and distribute food. Whatever horrible things may await human-ity in the years to come, global starvation is unlikely to be among them—though, as is the case with all of these beneficial technologies, making sure nobody's left behind could prove to be a challenge.

THE END OF PRIVACY?

In November 2016, WikiLeaks—the underground nonprofit founded by the curmudgeonly Australian hacker-activist Julian Assange (1971–)—arguably changed the outcome of the US presidential elec-tion by leaking private emails sent by members of the Democratic National Committee (DNC) to donors, family members, and each other. It was a much bigger scandal, in terms of its impact and scale, than the Watergate hotel burglary ordeal that had brought down US President Richard Nixon (1913–1994) just four decades earlier. But it's unlikely that most of the people involved in the hacking effort will ever be brought to trial, because most of the information was leaked in a relatively untraceable way.

The DNC was far from the first victim of this sort of untraceable hacking. Illicit nude photographs of numerous celebrities, stolen from their private messages, can be found in numerous dark corners of the Internet. The phrase "celebrity sex tape" has become such a cliché that the career impact of having one's private sex tape leaked to the public has become almost negligible. But it's not just our genitals that are liable to end up on the computer screens of strangers; almost anything we post on almost any website or service can potentially become public information at any time. Good encryption software can reduce, but not eliminate, this risk. And when governments collect this data, it could give them unparalleled power.

Now add in the fact that cameras and microphones keep getting smaller—there are now wireless cameras the size of a pea, and wireless microphones the size of a toothpick. How long will we be able to keep our secrets? And what will it mean for humanity when we can't?

The Future of Democracy

One of the reasons Fukuyama was so ready to declare the end of history is because liberal democracy *seems* like the natural endpoint of policy reform, but as CNN and *Washington Post* journalist Fareed Zakaria points out in *The Future of Freedom* (2003), the promise of democracy for the majority in a specific election means little if voting rights no longer exist in *future* elections: "It would be one man, one vote, one time."

While Western nations have expanded the franchise in recent decades to include women and people of color, and more countries hold elections than at any time in the past, this remains a dangerous time for democracy. Electronic vote tampering, voter suppression laws, impractically long voting lines, voter intimidation, partisan media control, gerrymandering (the drawing up of districts designed to underrepresent the votes of minority groups), and the outright arrest and prosecution of political opponents have transformed many former democracies into autocracies or near-autocracies. One particularly striking case is Russia, where President Vladimir Putin has essentially made himself dictator for life by routinely ordering the arrest and/or execution of his critics.

The ease with which nations slip in and out of "democratic" systems suggests that liberal democracy isn't so much a status that a nation achieves as it is a process, and one that requires constant vigilance. If we ever reach what Fukuyama called the end of history, our own complacency may bring history back with a vengeance.

INDEX

ABOUT THE AUTHOR

Tom Head is an interdisciplinary historian who specializes in the history of religion, ethics, and ideas. He holds a PhD in religion and society from Edith Cowan University and is author or coauthor of twenty-eight nonfiction books on a wide range of topics, including Oneworld's *Civil Liberties: A Beginner's Guide*, the University Press of Mississippi's *Conversations with Carl Sagan*, and Que/Pearson's *The Absolute Beginner's Guide to the Bible*. He served for nine years as About.com's guide to civil liberties, and currently writes videos on philosophy and pop culture for Wisecrack, LLC, a popular *YouTube* channel with over 1.5 million subscribers and more than 125 million views.